2⁰

3.1

Hello, Reader!

Welcome back to school. In this book, you will travel into the secret world of a Lost and Found and bravely climb to the top of a waterfall. You will also find out why a special quilt is important to one family.

As you read, look out for Dogzilla's doggy breath, and be prepared for dogs that turn into ducks.

**Let your mind travel.
Let the Rewards be yours!**

HOUGHTON MIFFLIN

Reading

Rewards

Senior Authors
J. David Cooper
John J. Pikulski

Authors
Patricia A. Ackerman
Kathryn H. Au
David J. Chard
Gilbert G. Garcia
Claude N. Goldenberg
Marjorie Y. Lipson
Susan E. Page
Shane Templeton
Sheila W. Valencia
MaryEllen Vogt

Consultants
Linda H. Butler
Linnea C. Ehri
Carla B. Ford

HOUGHTON MIFFLIN
Reading
A Legacy of Literacy

HOUGHTON MIFFLIN   BOSTON • MORRIS PLAINS, NJ

California • Colorado • Georgia • Illinois • New Jersey • Texas

Cover and title page photography by Tony Scarpetta.

Cover illustration is from *Raising Dragons,* by Jerdine Nolen, illustrated by Elise Primavera. Text copyright © 1998 by Jerdine Nolen. Illustrations copyright © 1998 by Elise Primavera. Reprinted by permission of Harcourt Inc. All rights reserved.

Acknowledgments begin on page 383.

Copyright © 2003 by Houghton Mifflin Company. All rights reserved.

Printed in the U.S.A.

ISBN: 0-618-25930-9

10 11 12 13 14 15 - DW - 11 10 09 08 07 06 05 04

Off to Adventure! 10

Reader's Library

- The Lunch Room
- Sacagawea
- A Great Day for Snorkeling

Theme Paperbacks

The Bravest Cat!
by Laura Driscoll

Blaze and the Forest Fire
by C. W. Anderson

Abigail's Drum
by John A. Minahan

4

Contents
Theme 2

Celebrating Traditions

124

Reader's Library

- Grandma's Table
- The Mask Makers
- The Weaver's Gift
- Festival in Valencia

Theme Paperbacks

The Best Older Sister
by Sook Nyul Choi

Century Farm
by Cris Peterson

Los Ojos del Tejedor: The Eyes of the Weaver
by Cristina Ortega

Focus on

Trickster Tales

Contents
Theme 3

Incredible STORIES

256

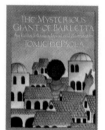

fantasy

Reader's Library

Incredible STORIES

- Robocat
- The Dragon of Krakow
- My Green Thumb
- Luna

Theme Paperbacks

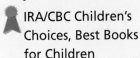

Mouse Soup

by Arnold Lobel

IRA/CBC Children's Choices, Best Books for Children

Mufaro's Beautiful Daughters

by John Steptoe

ALA Notable Children's Book, Caldecott Honor Book, Coretta Scott King Award

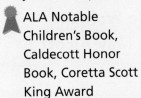

Charlotte's Web

by E. B. White

Newbery Honor Award, ALA Notable Children's Books 1940–1970

Off to Adventure!

Can't keep still all day....
I like adventures, and
I'm going to find one.

from *Little Women*
by Louisa May Alcott

Off to Adventure!

Contents

Student Writing Model

 Taking Tests

Reader's Library

- **The Lunch Room**
- **Sacagawea**
- **A Great Day for Snorkeling**

Theme Paperbacks

The Bravest Cat!
by Laura Driscoll
illustrated by DyAnne
DiSalvo-Ryan

Blaze and the Forest Fire
written and illustrated by C. W. Anderson

Abigail's Drum
by John A. Minahan
illustrations by Robert Quackenbush

Book Links

If you like . . .

The Lost and Found
by Mark Teague

If you like . . .

The Ballad of Mulan
by Song Nan Zhang

Then try . . .

The Secret Shortcut

by Mark Teague (Scholastic)
Wendell and Floyd hope their secret shortcut will help them arrive at school on time.

Sable

by Karen Hesse (Holt)
Tate must find a way to keep her dog, Sable, from wandering off and causing trouble.

Then try . . .

The Drums of Noto Hanto

by J. Alison James (DK)
The people of an ancient Japanese village drive off enemy forces.

The Adventures of Sparrowboy

by Brian Pinkney (Simon)
Henry the paperboy suddenly finds that he has become a flying superhero.

The Waterfall
by Jonathan London

Then try . . .

Hurricane!

by Jonathan London (Lothrop)
Two boys experience a fierce hurricane in Puerto Rico.

The Boxcar Children and the Mystery in San Francisco

by Gertrude Chandler Warner (Whitman)

The Alden children find adventure and solve a mystery when they visit their aunt and uncle.

Technology

At Education Place

Post your reviews of these books or see what others had to say.

www.eduplace.com/kids

. . .

At school

Read at school and take a quiz.

Accelerated Reader®

. . .

At home

Read at home and log on to

www.bookadventure.org

Have You Seen the Lost and Found?

If you've lost something in a store or at school, don't get **worried**. Just try asking for **directions** to the lost and found. A lost and found is a place to keep lost items until owners come to find them.

A visit to the lost and found can be an **unusual** adventure. Often the items are **visible** on shelves or tables. In other **situations**, the items may be tucked away in drawers or bins. Like the children in the story you are about to read, you may need to dig through piles of toys, shoes, or **rumpled** clothes to find what you're looking for. Be careful, though. You don't want to get lost yourself!

Meet the Author and Illustrator
Mark Teague

Mark Teague was always losing things when he was a kid. No surprise, then, that he often visited the lost and found at his school. He also thought that looking through the piles of lost toys and clothes was a lot of fun! Now you'll have a chance to see how Teague turned these real-life trips to the lost and found into an adventure story.

Other books:

Pigsty

Baby Tamer

The Secret Shortcut

How I Spent My Summer Vacation

Internet

Find out more about Mark Teague and his adventures by visiting Education Place.

www.eduplace.com/kids

18

the LOST and FOUND

mark teague

Strategy Focus

This adventure story has many twists and turns. When something surprising happens, stop and **summarize** to keep track of what you've read so far.

19

Wendell and Floyd were in trouble. That morning a giant squid had trapped them in the boys' restroom for almost an hour, causing them to miss a math test. Their teacher, Ms. Gernsblatt, had been furious.

"We have no luck," said Floyd.

Just then, Mona Tudburn entered the office. Mona was the new girl in their class.

"I'm trying to find the Lost and Found," she said. "I lost my lucky hat."

Wendell and Floyd glanced at each other. "That's strange," said Wendell. "We were just talking about luck."

"We don't have any," Floyd said.

"Neither do I," said Mona. "At least not without my hat."

21

Wendell pointed to a bin marked LOST AND FOUND. "I wish I had a lucky hat."

"So do I," Floyd agreed. "Then maybe we wouldn't get into these crazy situations."

Mona leaned farther and farther into the bin. Soon only her feet were visible. A moment later she was gone.

The boys walked over to have a closer look.

"Where did she go?" asked Wendell.

"I don't know," Floyd said. "She must be lost."

"Don't be silly," Wendell told him. "How can you get lost in the Lost and Found?"

Floyd looked at the principal's door and thought about all
the trouble they would be in if they weren't there when they
were called. "I guess we should go in after her," he sighed.

They climbed into the bin and instantly plunged into a deep well of lost toys and clothing.

"Look, Floyd, we found Mona."

"I think I found you," Mona said.

"Maybe we should get back now," Floyd suggested.

Mona noticed a sign pointing to a narrow passageway.
HAT ROOM, it read. "I bet my hat's in there."

"It couldn't hurt to look," said Wendell.

"Wait," warned Floyd. "What if we get lost?"

But Wendell and Mona laughed. "You can't get lost
in the Lost and Found."

The passageway led to a cave where a deep lake gurgled
and steamed. "I wonder if the principal knows this is here,"
said Floyd.

Wendell examined a suit of armor. "Some of this stuff has
been lost a long time."

"I still don't see my hat," grumbled Mona.
Then Wendell found a boat. "Perfect! We'll paddle across."

On the far side of the lake were three tunnels. "Which way do we go now?" asked Floyd.

"We could flip a coin," Wendell suggested.

Mona frowned. "That only works if there are two choices. Here we have three."

The boys thought about that for a while. Finally Wendell threw up his hands. "Let's try the middle one."

The tunnel became a winding hallway full of doors. They opened each one without finding a single hat. "I knew we would get lost," Floyd muttered.

34

"You can't get lost in the Lost and Found," Mona and
Wendell told him, but they no longer sounded so sure.

They came to one last door. Mona turned the knob
and pulled . . .

"The Hat Room!" cried the boys.

But Mona shook her head in dismay. "There's too many! I'll never find my hat in here."

They decided to look anyway. "Is it this one?" asked Wendell. It wasn't.

"How about this one?" Floyd held up a huge pink hat with purple flowers and a canary.

"Of course not," said Mona.

The boys began trying on hats themselves. "How do you tell if one is lucky?" Floyd asked.

"I don't know," said Mona. "It'll just sort of feel lucky."

Wendell tried on a burgundy fez with a small gold tassel. "This one feels lucky."

While Floyd was finding his own lucky hat, Wendell's tassel began to tickle his nose. "I think I'm going to sneeze."

"Hold on. I'll get you a tissue." Mona reached into her purse, and when she did, a strange look came over her face. She held up something green and badly rumpled.

"My lucky hat. I guess it was in my purse all along."

For a moment, nobody spoke. Then Floyd sighed, "At least we can go back now."

"Maybe not," Wendell said.

"What do you mean?" asked Floyd and Mona.

"I mean, we might be lost."

Floyd groaned. "I thought you said we couldn't get lost in the Lost and Found."

"It's been an unusual day," said Wendell. "To be honest,
I don't even remember which door we came through."

The children looked around. There were doorways in
all directions. None of them could remember which one
was theirs.

Suddenly Mona laughed. "What are we worried about? We've all got our lucky hats, right?"

She closed her eyes and turned slowly around. When she opened them again, she pointed straight ahead. "I say we go that way."

After a long journey, the children's heads popped out of the Lost and Found bin, just in time to hear the principal call, "Wendell and Floyd, come in here please."

It was late that afternoon before the boys left school.
They found their new friend Mona waiting for them.

"How was it?" she asked.

"Not bad," said Floyd.

The principal had merely lectured them about telling the truth. Of course, Ms. Gernsblatt had made them stay and finish their math tests, but it could have been worse.

"I think our luck is changing," said Wendell.

Mona nodded. "Me too."

Since it was late, they decided to take a shortcut.

"I hope we don't get lost," said Floyd, but he wasn't really worried. Neither were Mona and Wendell. They paused for a moment to put on their hats. Then they all started home, feeling lucky together.

Think About the Selection

1. Does luck have anything to do with Wendell and Floyd's troubles? Give reasons for your answer.

2. Why do the boys follow Mona into the Lost and Found bin?

3. Why do you think the world of the Lost and Found becomes stranger as the children go deeper into it?

4. What might have happened if the children hadn't gotten out of the Lost and Found when they did?

5. Would you have followed Mona into the Lost and Found? Why or why not?

6. **Connecting/Comparing** What makes *The Lost and Found* an adventure? How do the illustrations make you feel as if *you* are part of the adventure too?

Explaining

Write Instructions

Now that you know the way, write step-by-step instructions for getting out of the Lost and Found. Start at the room right after the long fall through the Lost and Found bin.

Tips

- **Number the steps of your instructions.**
- **Use command words such as *turn* and *follow*.**

Math

Work with Probability

Help the children choose one of the three tunnels. With a partner, make a spinner that gives each tunnel an equal chance of being picked. Spin it thirty times. Record how many times each tunnel comes up. Compare your results with the rest of the class.

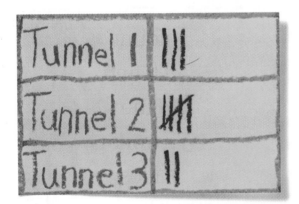

Bonus Make a spinner that gives one tunnel a greater chance of being picked than the other two. Spin it thirty times. Compare your results to the first thirty spins.

Art

Draw a Room

Which room in *The Lost and Found* would you have liked to go into? Go back through the story. Choose a room you see there or create a new room that isn't shown in the illustrations. Draw the room and the things you might find in it.

Solve a Web Mystery Grid

Follow the instructions and find a picture that's been lost in the dots. Visit Education Place and print out a mystery grid.

www.eduplace.com/kids

Skill: How to Read a Poem

- Read the poem several times. Try reading the poem aloud.

- Listen for patterns, such as rhythm or rhyme.

- Think about the idea the poet is trying to express.

I Lost the Work I Found

Today
I lost
the
work
I found
in
the
lost
and
found
yesterday.

Tomorrow
in
the
lost
and
found
I'll find
the
work
I lost
today
after
I found
it
yesterday.

Kalli Dakos

Lost

I cannot find my basketball.
I cannot find my locker.
I cannot find my homework,
which is really quite a shocker.

I cannot find my lunch box.
Worse, I cannot find my classes.
I'm going to have a rotten day
until I find my glasses.

Bruce Lansky

September Yearning

Daddy hands me a shirt of many blues
And I've polished my sturdy shoes
And Mama's pressed my overalls
For the very first day of school falls
   in September

I reach for new books
And read about old heroes
I compute numbers
I calculate zeros

Then pages of poems I memorize
And paint the pictures
Behind my eyes

Joyce Carol Thomas

A Personal Narrative

A personal narrative is a true story about something that happened to the writer. Use this student's writing as a model when you write a personal narrative of your own.

A good **beginning** makes the reader want to read on to find out what will happen.

Lost Shoes

Come on! Want to read about me losing my shoes? It was March 6, 1999. My friend Lindsey came over to play. She liked my shoes, and I liked hers, so we traded. A little later it was time for her to go home. I waved good-bye through my window as she walked away. The next morning my shoes were gone! I was as sad as a mother whose child is lost. Man, where could they be? I looked all over my room, but all I found was an old piece of pizza half eaten by ants. Ewwwww!

The first thing I did was to look through the whole house. But all I found was a dirty sock, 3 candy bars, an old map, and 15 pieces of paper. Next, I looked in the car but all I found was an old box,

6 watches, 7 candy wrappers, and a piece of cheese. I thought and looked and wondered where they could be.

Finally, I retraced my steps and remembered trading shoes with Lindsey. Then I zoomed to her house and asked for my shoes back. I was as relieved as a mother whose child has been found. I cleaned my shoes all day and man did they shine!

When I dressed for school the next day, I proudly tied the laces of my shiny blue shoes. I reached for my backpack but. . . . OH NO! WHERE'S MY BACKPACK???

Including **details** makes the narrative real for a reader.

It's important to keep to the **topic**.

A good **ending** pleases a reader.

Meet the Author

Nina M.
Grade: three
State: Florida
Hobbies: writing, reading, and playing with her sister
What she'd like to be when she grows up: an artist and musician

The Mulan Legend

An old Chinese legend tells the story of a young woman named Mulan. Many years ago, there was much war and fighting in China. China's leader, the Emperor, often drafted men to join the army. These men would say **farewell** to their families and leave home to serve with their **comrades**.

Sometimes the army would win a battle and return home **triumphant**. At other times, the men would not be **victorious**, even though they had bravely **endured** much hardship.

The old legend says that Mulan showed great courage during these difficult times. The story you are about to read retells the legend of how Mulan became a hero to the Chinese people.

These sculptures show how the Emperor's **troops** would put on **armor** to protect themselves.

54

This clay sculpture shows what an army horse might have looked like.

This building sits on a cliff high above the Yellow River in China, where the troops might have camped long ago.

MEET THE
AUTHOR AND ILLUSTRATOR
Song Nan Zhang

- Song Nan Zhang was born in Shanghai, China, in 1942.

- Once, when Mr. Zhang was a small child, he saw a baby tiger hiding in some plants outside his family's house. He ran into the kitchen and shouted, "Mom, Mom, there's a big cat outside!"

- As a young boy, Mr. Zhang drew some silly pictures of his father and hung them on a wall at home. Instead of getting angry, his father was proud that his son was such a good artist!

- Today, Mr. Zhang lives in Canada, where he works as an artist, author, and teacher.

OTHER BOOKS:

The Children of China
Cowboy on the Steppes

The Legend of the Panda
(by Linda Granfield)

The Man Who Made Paris
(by Frieda Wishinsky)

Learn more about Song Nan Zhang by visiting Education Place.

www.eduplace.com/kids

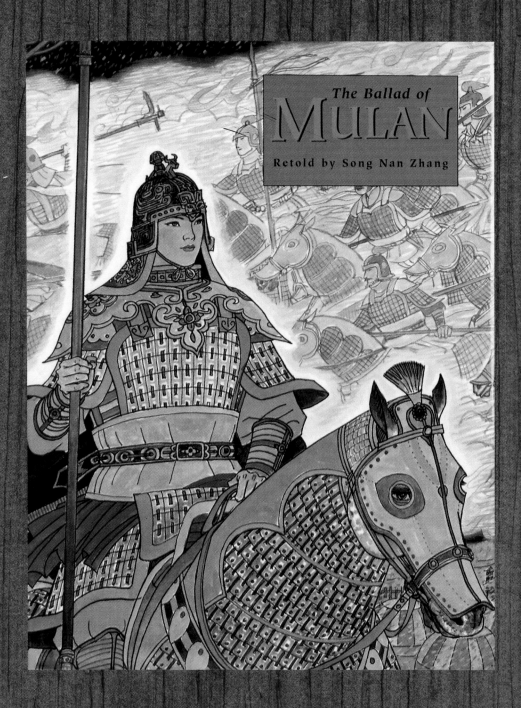

The Ballad of
MULAN
Retold by Song Nan Zhang

Strategy Focus

As you read, **monitor** how well you understand
the events in the story. Reread to **clarify** anything
that seems unclear.

Long ago, in a village in northern China, there lived a girl named Mulan. One day, she sat at her loom weaving cloth. *Click-clack! Click-clack!* went the loom.

唧唧復唧唧

木蘭當戶織

不聞機杼聲

惟聞女嘆息

問女何所思

問女何所憶

女亦無所思

女亦無所憶

Suddenly, the sound of weaving changed to sorrowful sighs.
"What troubles you?" her mother asked.
"Nothing, Mother," Mulan softly replied.

59

昨晚見軍帖可汗大點兵

木蘭辭　北朝樂府

Her mother asked her again and again, until Mulan
finally said, "There is news of war."

軍書十二卷卷卷有爺名

木蘭辭　北朝樂府

"Invaders are attacking. The Emperor is calling for
troops. Last night, I saw the draft poster and twelve scrolls
of names in the market. Father's name is on every one."

61

阿爺無大児木蘭無長兄

木蘭辭　北朝樂府

"But Father is old and frail," Mulan sighed.
"How can he fight? He has no grown son and I have
no elder brother."

願為市鞍馬從此替爺征

木蘭辭　北朝樂府

"I will go to the markets. I shall buy a saddle and
a horse. I must fight in Father's place."

東市買駿馬西市買鞍韉

木蘭辭　北朝樂府

From the eastern market Mulan bought a horse, and
from the western market, a saddle. From the southern market
she bought a bridle, and from the northern market, a whip.

南市買轡頭北市買長鞭

木蘭辭　北朝樂府

At dawn Mulan dressed in her armor and bid a sad
farewell to her father, mother, sister, and brother. Then
she mounted her horse and rode off with the soldiers.

朝辭爺娘去暮宿黃河邊

木蘭辭　北朝樂府

By nightfall she was camped by the bank of
the Yellow River. She thought she heard her mother
calling her name.

但聞黃河流水鳴濺濺
不聞爺娘喚女聲

木蘭辭　北朝樂府

But it was only the sound of the river crying.

旦辭黃河去暮至黑山頭

木蘭辭　北朝樂府

At sunrise Mulan took leave of the Yellow River.
At dusk she reached the peak of Black Mountain.

不聞爺娘喚女聲　但聞燕山胡騎聲啾啾

木蘭辭　北朝樂府

In the darkness she longed to hear her father's voice but heard only the neighing of enemy horses far away.

萬里赴戎機關山度若飛

木蘭辭　北朝樂府

Mulan rode ten thousand miles to fight a hundred battles.
She crossed peaks and passes like a bird in flight.

70

朔氣傳金柝寒光照鐵衣

木蘭辭　北朝樂府

Nights at the camp were harsh and cold, but
Mulan endured every hardship. Knowing her father
was safe warmed her heart.

将軍百戰死

木蘭辭 北朝樂府

The war dragged on. Fierce battles ravaged the land.
One after another, noble generals lost their lives.

壮士十年歸

木蘭辭　北朝樂府

Mulan's skill and courage won her respect and rank. After ten years, she returned as a great general, triumphant and victorious!

歸来見天子天子坐明堂

木蘭辭　北朝樂府

The Emperor summoned Mulan to the High Palace.
He praised her for her bravery and leadership in battle.

策勛十二轉賞賜百千強

木蘭辭　北朝樂府

The Court would bestow many great titles upon her.
Mulan would be showered with gifts of gold.

木蘭不用尚書郎
可汗問所欲

木蘭辭

北朝樂府

"Worthy General, you may have your heart's desire,"
the Emperor said.

"I have no need for honors or gold," Mulan replied.

願借明駝千里足　送兒還故鄉

木蘭辭　北朝樂府

"All I ask for is a swift camel to take me back home."
The Emperor sent a troop to escort Mulan on her trip.

阿姊聞妹來當戶理紅妝
爺娘聞女來出郭相扶將

In town, the news of Mulan's return created great
excitement. Holding each other, her proud parents
walked to the village gate to welcome her.

78

小弟聞姊來　磨刀霍霍向猪羊

木蘭辭　北朝樂府

Waiting at home, Mulan's sister beautified herself.
Her brother sharpened his knife to prepare a pig and
sheep for the feast in Mulan's honor.

木蘭辭　北朝樂府

脫我戰時袍
著我舊時裳
開我東閣門
坐我西閣床

Home at last! Mulan threw open her bedroom door and smiled. She removed her armor and changed into one of her favorite dresses.

當窗理雲鬢對鏡貼花黃

木蘭辭　北朝樂府

She brushed out her shiny black hair and pasted
a yellow flower on her face. She looked into the
mirror and smiled again, happy to be home.

木蘭辭　北朝樂府

出門看伙伴伙伴皆惊惶

What a surprise it was when Mulan appeared at
the door! Her comrades were astonished and amazed.
"How is this possible?" they asked.

同行十二年　不知木蘭是女郎

木蘭辭　北朝樂府

"How could we have fought side by side with you
for ten years and not have known you were a woman!"

雄兔腳撲朔雌兔眼迷離

木蘭辭

北朝樂府

Mulan replied, "They say the male rabbit likes to hop and leap, while the female rabbit prefers to sit still. But in times of danger, when the two rabbits scurry by, who can tell male from female?"

雙兔傍地走安能辯我是雄雌

木蘭辭 北朝樂府

Mulan's glory spread through the land. And to this day, we sing of this brave woman who loved her family and served her country, asking for nothing in return.

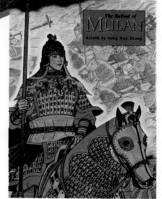

Think About the Selection

1. Why doesn't Mulan tell her mother right away that there is news of war?

2. What might have happened if Mulan had asked to fight dressed as a female soldier?

3. Why are the men who fought side by side with Mulan so surprised that she is a woman? List more than one reason.

4. What do Mulan's actions teach you about the meaning of courage?

5. The story of Mulan has been retold for hundreds of years. Why do you think people enjoy retelling it?

6. **Connecting/Comparing** Which do you think is a more exciting adventure story, *The Lost and Found* or *The Ballad of Mulan*? Why?

Expressing

Write a Letter

May 23

Dear Father,

Mulan spent many nights away from home. Write a letter from Mulan to her father. Tell him what it's like where Mulan is and what she has been doing since she left home.

Tips
- **Use vivid words to describe people, places, and events.**
- **Remember to use the five parts of a letter.**

Make a Leadership Award

We know that Mulan was a good soldier. In a small group, discuss other ways Mulan was a good leader. Then discuss people who are good leaders in your community. Vote for the best leader. Make a leadership award for the winner. Write his or her name on the award.

Compare the Book and a Movie

Now that you've read *The Ballad of Mulan,* you may want to compare this version of the story to a movie version. Use a Venn diagram to list what is the same and what is different. Then choose one scene that was much better in either the movie or the book and discuss it with a classmate.

Internet

Post a Review

Tell other students around the country what you think of *The Ballad of Mulan.* Write a review of the story and post it on Education Place.

www.eduplace.com/kids

Chinese

Skill: How to
Read a Key

*A key is a chart
that tells what
symbols mean.*

Before you read . . .

① **Look** at the
key to see what
information it
gives you.

② **Predict** how you
will use the key.

While you read . . .

① **Look back** at the
key to match the
symbols you find
in the text.

② **Identify** the
meaning of
each symbol.

Are you a 子 or a 女 or a 人? Do you wake with the 日 or the 月? Have you ever ridden in a 車 up a 山 in the 雨? Unless you read Chinese, you probably don't know the answers to these questions — yet!

Chinese writing is made up of pictures called characters. A long time ago, these pictures looked like the things they stood for. For example, ⊙ was the picture for "sun," and ☽ was the picture for "moon." See the round sun and the half-moon? But over the centuries, the characters changed until they now look like 日 (sun) and 月 (moon). Imagine: over one billion people use this beautiful writing.

Read the story on page 91. See if you can figure out the meanings of the Chinese characters. The words and characters in the box will help you.

the Write Way

by Susan Wills
illustrated by
Lily Toy Hong

cart

mountain

child

rain

fire

sun

man

woman

moon

車 cart	人 man	日 sun
子 child	山 mountain	女 woman
火 fire	雨 rain	月 moon

On top of a 山 there lived a 人, a 女, and a 子. Every day when the 日 came up, they took their 車 and walked down the 山 to the market for food. Every night when the 月 rose, they walked back up the 山 to their home to eat supper.

After many years, the family grew very tired of all that walking up and down. "If only we had 雨 so that we could raise our own food," the 女 said.

Then one night, the 子 had a dream. The next morning when the 日 came up, the 子 went outside and started a 火 with some sticks. Since there had never been a 火 on top of the 山 before, the clouds were frightened and sent down 雨 to put the 火 out. From then on, anytime the family wanted 雨, one of them would start a small 火, and the clouds would hurry to put it out.

Soon the family had enough water to grow a fine vegetable garden. Of course, now the 子, the 女, and the 人 were all pretty tired of weeding vegetables and chasing rabbits from their garden. So one morning, when the 日 came up, they took their 車 and walked down the 山 to the market for food.

Now that you've read the story, why not make up your own tale using the same Chinese characters? When you've finished your tale, give it to a friend to read!

What Is a Waterfall?

A sudden drop in the level of a river or stream causes water to fall over an edge. This is called a waterfall. Some waterfalls are only a few feet high. Others, like the one in the next story, plunge over cliffs and crash down into deep **canyons**

Running water can cut rock shelves called **ledges** out of **sheer** canyon walls.

Water crashes down, creating a foamy pool that may look like a boiling **cauldron**.

Boulders are often found in or near a riverbed.

Very tiny waterfalls that are close together are called **rapids**.

When hiking, areas near a waterfall should be scouted for the safest path.

The WATERFALL

by
Jonathan London

illustrated by
Jill Kastner

Strategy Focus

The family in this story enjoys exploring the outdoors. Read carefully and try to **predict** what they will see and do next.

It was the middle of July when we drove way up into the mountains and backpacked up a creek.

95

The banks were lined with poison oak, so we waded through the cold water — hip deep for my parents, chest deep for us — our backpacks balanced on our heads.

We set up camp on a sandy flat beside a pool in a ring of boulders. What a swimming hole! My brother and I swam, diving and tumbling in the diamond-clear water.

We hiked farther upstream, against little rapids, picking our way among slippery boulders. Suddenly we heard a roaring sound, and as we came around a bend, we saw what was causing it.

A huge waterfall! It rose high above us, higher than the tallest pines. Only a few wet ferns clung to the steep rock slope. A rainbow glowed in the roaring mist.

"Wow!" I said. "Let's climb it!"

"No way," said Dad. "End of the road."

We turned back, and that night we had a cookout, and watched the sparks climb to the stars. I couldn't stop thinking about the waterfall — and how much I'd like to climb it.

Later, snuggled in my bag, I heard a growl, and a rustle in the brush . . . then finally fell asleep, a little scared.

101

In the morning we found tracks. "A mountain lion," said Dad. "It must have come down for water."

It made my heart feel big and wild, like when I saw the waterfall. "Let's go climb the falls!" I said.

"It can't be done," said Dad, "but let's go anyhow!"

The sun was hot as a bonfire. We cut leaves of Indian rhubarb as wide as elephants' ears, and tied them on our heads with vine to keep us cool. Then we waded against the little rapids deep into the canyon.

I was the first one to the waterfall. "Let's go up," I said.

My brother grinned. "If *you* go, *I* will," he said.

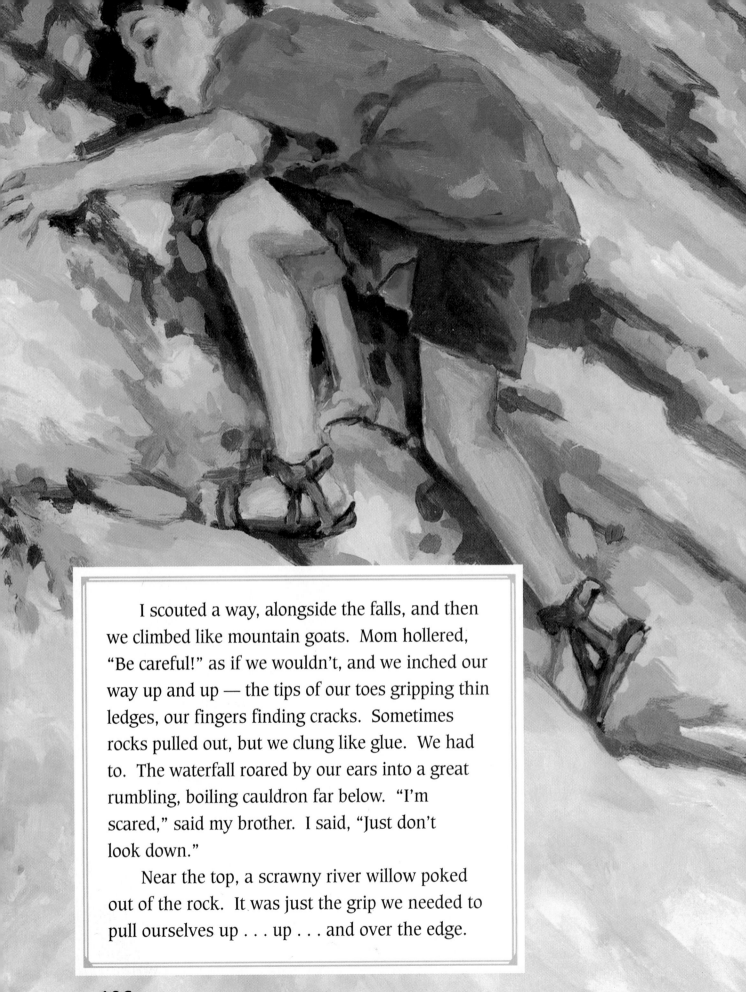

I scouted a way, alongside the falls, and then
we climbed like mountain goats. Mom hollered,
"Be careful!" as if we wouldn't, and we inched our
way up and up — the tips of our toes gripping thin
ledges, our fingers finding cracks. Sometimes
rocks pulled out, but we clung like glue. We had
to. The waterfall roared by our ears into a great
rumbling, boiling cauldron far below. "I'm
scared," said my brother. I said, "Just don't
look down."

Near the top, a scrawny river willow poked
out of the rock. It was just the grip we needed to
pull ourselves up . . . up . . . and over the edge.

When we stood at the top, we slapped five and shouted down, "HEY MOM, DAD! IT'S LIKE A WHOLE OTHER WORLD UP HERE! COME ON UP! YOU CAN DO IT!" And I did a little dance.

Mom looked at Dad, Dad looked at Mom. Then Mom started climbing, and Dad followed — I couldn't believe my eyes!

I lay on my belly and shouted directions. "No, not *that* ledge — try the one up to your right!" I never felt more anxious — seeing my parents clinging to that sheer rock — or more proud, either.

Then I heard a shout and my heart jumped into my mouth.

But it was a shout of triumph! My folks pulled themselves up, up, and over the top.

"We *did* it!" Mom beamed, breathing hard.

"You *did* it!" I echoed. "Dad, I thought you said it couldn't be done!"

"It *can't,*" he said, grinning like a grizzly bear.

Then all together, we continued upstream.

"Look!" I shouted.

A big piece of driftwood was wedged between boulders.

"It looks just like a dancer!"

It was river-smooth, polished by water. It looked like a boy whirling around in joy.

"Can we take it home?" I asked. "As a kind of souvenir?"

"If you can carry it," said Dad, "you can keep it."

It was about the hardest thing I ever did, but I lugged that heavy driftwood back out. . . .

112

And now it stands in our yard.
Some people think it's a sculpture.
We just call it "The Dancer." Whenever
I look at it, it reminds me of the
waterfall — and makes my heart feel
big and wild.

Meet the Author
Jonathan London

Birthday: March 11

An adventure he had as a boy: London's father was in the United States Navy, so the family moved many times while London was growing up. He has lived all over the United States and in Puerto Rico.

How he became a writer: When London's children were young, he began making up stories to tell them. He wrote one down, and it became the book *The Owl Who Became the Moon.*

Hobbies: Writing poetry, hiking, backpacking, cross-country skiing, dancing

Other books: *Hip Cat, Red Wolf Country, Hurricane!, Thirteen Moons on Turtle's Back* (with Joseph Bruchac)

Meet the Illustrator
Jill Kastner

Where she lives: Weehawken, New Jersey
Her husband's name: Tim
Pets: Three cats

Other books: *Barnyard Big Top* (which she also wrote), *Down at Angel's* (by Sharon Chmielarz), *Howling Hill* (by Will Hobbs)

Discover more about Jonathan London and Jill Kastner by visiting Education Place. **www.eduplace.com/kids**

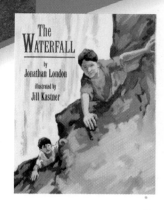

Think About the Selection

1. How can you tell that the family in this story enjoys being together? Find clues in the story.

2. The boy's heart feels "big and wild" when he sees the tracks of the mountain lion. What do you think this means?

3. Why do you think the father changes his mind about letting the boys climb the waterfall?

4. Why is "The Dancer" important to the boy?

5. What parts of this family's trip would you have liked or not liked? What activities do you enjoy with your family?

6. **Connecting/Comparing** At the end of his adventure, the boy goes home feeling very different. Mulan is different when she returns home too. Compare their experiences.

Describing

Write a Description

The waterfall is a special place for the boy in the story. Write a description of an outdoor place that you enjoy visiting. Use details that will help someone who has never been to your place understand what it is like.

Tips

- Draw a picture of your place to help you remember details.
- Use words that describe what you see, hear, and smell.

Science

Make a Diagram

Use the picture on pages 100–101 to help you draw a diagram of the waterfall in the story. Clearly label the canyon walls, ledges, pool, boulders, and rapids. If you need help, reread pages 92–93.

Listening and Speaking

Listen to Your World

Go back through the selection. Find all the sounds the boy hears during his trip. Now open your ears to the world around you! Choose a place such as a classroom, a park, a street corner, or your home. Listen carefully for five minutes. Write down what you hear.

Tips

- **Stay quiet and still while you listen.**
- **Close your eyes to make listening easier.**

Internet

Take an Online Poll

Have you ever gone backpacking? Have you ever seen a waterfall? Take an online poll at Education Place.

www.eduplace.com/kids

Skill: How to Read a Map

❶ Use the **compass rose** to find north, south, east, and west.

❷ Read the **labels** to find cities, states, countries, and other places on the map.

❸ Find **symbols** such as shapes or lines that point out information.

Camping on the WILD Side!

story and photos by Roger Kaye

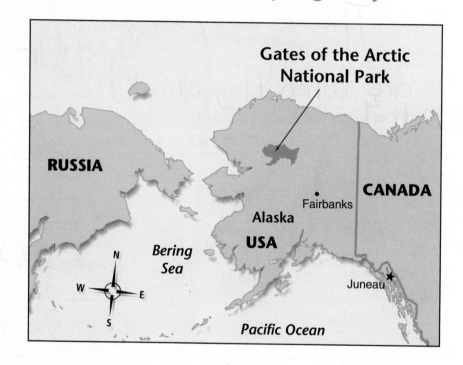

"We made it!" Lolly Andrews says to her sister, Polly. After a long hike to the top of a ridge, the 11-year-old twins and their parents slip off their backpacks.

Below, the Alatna River flows through a wide valley. This is the Gates of the Arctic National Park in Alaska (see map). No roads reach the remote park. The family flew there in Dad's small airplane from Fairbanks, some 200 miles (320 km) to the south.

Lolly and Polly spend a few days camping in the wild — but you'd never know they were there!

"It's as if we were the first people ever here!" Lolly says. The girls, who are half Yupik Eskimo, have been waiting a long time to make this trip. Now Polly has fun imagining they are explorers. She points up the valley to where the river disappears around a bend. "Wonder what we'll discover tomorrow. . . ."

Near the river, the girls find a flat, sandy area. They could camp there without disturbing anything. This family practices something called Leave-No-Trace Camping. And to the girls, it's like a game. "We try to leave our campsite looking as if no one had ever been there. It's a challenge — but it's fun!"

119

Leave-No-Trace Camping Tips

Wilderness areas are not all the same, so it's not always possible to follow the same rules everywhere. But here are some suggestions to keep in mind when you go to any wilderness area.

▲ If you find a campsite that's already established, use it. If you do set up a new campsite, try to make it where you won't disturb any plants.

▶ It's best to cook on a camping stove. If you do make a campfire, keep it small. If there's already a fire ring nearby, make your fire there. Always build campfires away from trees, grass, and other plants. Use only small pieces of dead wood found lying on the ground. Before you leave, fill in the fire pit with sand or soil to leave the spot just as you found it.

◀ After dinner, Mom asks the girls to do the dishes. They carry them to the river and fill them with wet sand. Why use sand instead of dishwashing soap? Soap has chemicals that can pollute the water. And sand works as a scrubber, so bits of food scrape off easily.

Before beginning the hike back to the plane, each girl grabs a twig and sweeps around where the tents and fire had been. Every trace melts away. "Now those who come here next can be explorers too," Polly says, "as if *they* were the first to discover it!"

✔ Choosing the Best Answer

Many tests have questions and a choice of three or four answers. How do you choose the best answer? Below is a sample test item for the selection *The Waterfall*. The correct answer is shown. Use the tips to help you answer this kind of test question.

Tips

- Read the directions carefully.
- Read the question and **all** the answer choices.
- Look back at the selection if you need to.
- Fill in the answer circle completely.
- After you finish a test, check your answers if you have time.

Read the question. Fill in the circle next to the best answer.

1   Why does the family walk in the creek at the beginning of the story?

○   They think it will be fun and exciting.

●   They don't want to walk through the poison oak that grows on the banks of the creek.

○   It's a hot day, and they want to cool off.

○   They are lost in the mountains.

Now see how one student figured out the best answer.

How do I choose the best answer? The answer should tell why the family walks **in** the creek.

The first three answers make sense, but I don't remember reading the first or the third ones in the story. The fourth answer is wrong because the family isn't lost.

The second answer makes sense, and I remember the boy telling about poison oak. The second answer is the correct one.

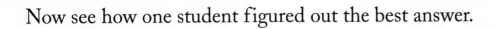

Celebrating Traditions

The town I live in, the street,
   the house, the room,
The pavement of the city,
   or a garden all in bloom,
The church, the school,
   the clubhouse,
The million lights I see,
   but especially the people —
That's America to me!

from the song
"The House I Live In"
lyrics by Lewis Allan

Statue of Liberty, 1986
Milton Bond

Celebrating Traditions

Contents

Reader's Library

- **Grandma's Table**
- **The Mask Makers**
- **The Weaver's Gift**
- **Festival in Valencia**

Theme Paperbacks

The Best Older Sister
by Sook Nyul Choi, illustrated by
Cornelius Van Wright and Ying-Hwa Hu

Century Farm
by Cris Peterson, photographs by Alvis Upitis

Los Ojos del Tejedor: The Eyes of the Weaver
by Cristina Ortega, illustrated by Patricio García

Book Links

If you like . . .

The Keeping Quilt
by Patricia Polacco

Then try . . .

Rechenka's Eggs
by Patricia Polacco (Philomel)

An injured goose named Rechenka lays some surprising eggs.

The Wedding
by Angela Johnson (Orchard)

Daisy feels excited, happy, and even a little sad at her sister's wedding.

If you like . . .

Anthony Reynoso: Born to Rope
by Ginger Gordon

Then try . . .

Easter Parade
by Eloise Greenfield (Hyperion)

Leanna and Elizabeth enjoy the Easter Parade even though war has made life hard for them.

Basket Moon
by Mary Lyn Ray (Little)

A boy continues his family's tradition of weaving baskets.

If you like . . .

The Talking Cloth
by Rhonda Mitchell

Then try . . .

Celebrating Chinese New Year
by Diane Hoyt-Goldsmith (Holiday)

In San Francisco, Ryan prepares to celebrate Chinese New Year.

Red Bird
by Barbara Mitchell (Lothrop)

Kate celebrates her Nanticoke traditions at a powwow in Delaware.

If you like . . .

Dancing Rainbows
by Evelyn Clarke Mott

Then try . . .

A Picnic in October
by Eve Bunting (Harcourt)

Every year, Tony's grandmother celebrates her birthday in the same unusual way.

Clambake
by Russell Peters (Lerner)

A Wampanoag boy learns how to prepare a clambake.

Technology

Visit **www.eduplace.com/kids** **Education Place®**

Read at school Accelerated Reader®

Read at home www.bookadventure.org

Book Adventure™

PATRICIA POLACCO
The Keeping Quilt

10TH ANNIVERSARY EDITION

Background and Vocabulary

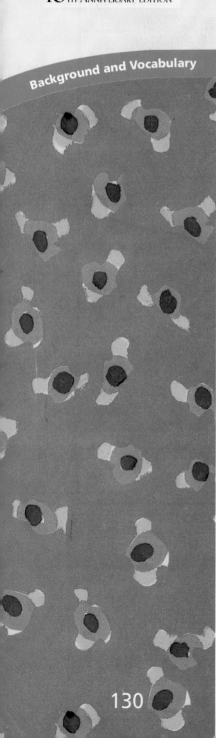

Quilts

A quilt is made of two layers of cloth **sewn** together using **needles** and thread. Quilt makers often use **scraps** of colorful old clothing to create designs. Sometimes they use large scraps to make a **border** around the edges of the quilt.

Many families have homemade quilts. Some families bring out their quilts only for a family **gathering**, such as a wedding or a birthday. Other people use their quilts every day. A family quilt, like the one in the selection you are about to read, helps people remember special times. It keeps them warm, inside and out.

1 Cut out shapes or designs.

2 Attach beads or buttons if you like.

3 Use threaded needles to sew on the shapes.

4 Enjoy your
finished quilt.

Meet the AUTHOR AND ILLUSTRATOR

Patricia Polacco

 When Patricia Polacco was a child her family spent many hours telling stories. Listening to them made Polacco want to share these wonderful stories with others. One of her favorite things to tell young writers is "LISTEN . . . LISTEN . . . LISTEN."

After college, Polacco lived in Australia, England, France, Russia, and California. Now Polacco lives on a farm in Michigan with her husband, her cats, two goats, and a lamb. Her grown children live about forty miles away and visit often.

Other Books

Chicken Sunday

My Rotten Redheaded Older Brother

Luba and the Wren

Thank You, Mr. Falker

Internet

There's more to learn about Patricia Polacco on Education Place. **www.eduplace.com/kids**

PATRICIA POLACCO
The Keeping Quilt

10TH ANNIVERSARY EDITION

Strategy Focus

As you read, **evaluate** how well Patricia Polacco helps you understand her feelings about her family's quilt and their traditions.

W hen my Great-Gramma Anna came to America, she wore the same thick overcoat and big boots she had worn for farm work. But her family weren't dirt farmers anymore. In New York City, her father's work was hauling things on a wagon, and the rest of the family made artificial flowers all day.

Everyone was in a hurry, and it was so crowded, not like backhome Russia. But all the same it was their home, and most of their neighbors were just like them.

When Anna went to school, English sounded to her like pebbles dropping into shallow water. *Shhhhhh . . . Shhhhhh . . . Shhhhhh.* In six months she was speaking English. Her parents almost never learned, so she spoke English for them, too.

The only things she had left of backhome Russia were her dress and babushka she liked to throw up into the air when she was dancing.

And her dress was getting too small. After her mother
had sewn her a new one, she took her old dress and babushka.
Then from a basket of old clothes she took Uncle Vladimir's shirt,
Aunt Havalah's nightdress, and an apron of Aunt Natasha's.

"We will make a quilt to help us always remember home,"
Anna's mother said. "It will be like having the family in backhome
Russia dance around us at night."

And so it was. Anna's mother invited all the neighborhood ladies. They cut out animals and flowers from the scraps of clothing. Anna kept the needles threaded and handed them to the ladies as they needed them. The border of the quilt was made of Anna's babushka.

On Friday nights Anna's mother would say the prayers that started the Sabbath. The family ate challah and chicken soup. The quilt was the tablecloth.

Anna grew up and fell in love with Great-Grandpa Sasha. To show he wanted to be her husband, he gave Anna a gold coin, a dried flower, and a piece of rock salt all tied into a linen

handkerchief. The gold was for wealth, the flower for love, and the salt so their lives would have flavor.

She accepted the hankie and they were engaged.

Under the wedding huppa, Anna and Sasha promised each other love and understanding. After the wedding, the men and women celebrated separately.

When my Grandma Carle was born, Anna wrapped her daughter in the quilt to welcome her warmly into the world. Carle was given a gift of gold, flower, salt, and bread. Gold so she would never know poverty, a flower so she would always know love, salt so her life would always have flavor, and bread so that she would never know hunger.

Carle learned to keep the Sabbath and to cook and clean and do washing.

"Married you'll be someday," Anna told Carle, and . . .

again the quilt became a wedding huppa, this time for Carle's wedding to Grandpa George. Men and women celebrated together, but they still did not dance together. In Carle's wedding bouquet were a gold coin, bread, and salt.

Carle and George moved to a farm in Michigan and Great-Gramma Anna came to live with them. The quilt once again wrapped a new little girl, Mary Ellen.

Mary Ellen called Anna, Lady Gramma. She had grown very old and was sick a lot of the time. The quilt kept her legs warm.

On Anna's ninety-eighth birthday, the cake was a kulich, a rich cake with raisins and candied fruit in it.

When Great-Gramma Anna died, prayers were said to lift her soul to heaven. My mother Mary Ellen was now grown up.

When Mary Ellen left home, she took the quilt with her.
When she became a bride, the quilt became her huppa. For
the first time, friends who were not Jews came to the wedding.
My mother wore a suit, but in her bouquet were gold, bread,
and salt.

The quilt welcomed me, Patricia, into the world . . . and
it was the tablecloth for my first birthday party.

At night, I would trace my fingers around the edges of each animal on the quilt before I went to sleep. I told my mother stories about the animals on the quilt. She told me whose sleeve had made the horse, whose apron had made the chicken, whose dress had made the flowers, and whose babushka went around the edge of the quilt.

The quilt was a pretend cape when I was in the bullring, or sometimes a tent in the steaming Amazon jungle.

At my wedding, men and women danced together. In my bouquet were gold, bread, and salt — and a sprinkle of grape juice, so I would always know laughter.

Many years ago I held Traci Denise in the quilt for the first time.

Three years later my mother held Steven John in the quilt for the first time. We were all so proud of Traci's new baby brother.

Just like their mother, grandmother, and great-grandmother before them, they, too, used the quilt to celebrate birthdays and make superhero capes.

As the years passed and Traci and Steven were growing up, their grandmother took pleasure at every family gathering to tell the story of the quilt. We all knew whose clothes made each flower and animal. My mother was lucky enough to show the wonder of this quilt to my brother's grandchildren, her great-grandchildren.

When my mother died, prayers were said to lift her soul to heaven. Traci and Steven were now all grown up and getting ready to start their own lives.

And now I wait . . . for the day that I, too, will be a grandmother, and tell the story of the Keeping Quilt to my grandbabies.

Responding

Think About the Selection

1. Why does Anna's mother start the tradition of the Keeping Quilt?

2. Compare each daughter's wedding to her mother's wedding. How is each wedding different and the same?

3. How do you think Patricia Polacco feels about her family? Give examples from the story.

4. What does the Keeping Quilt help the family keep? In what other ways might a family keep something?

5. Why do you think Polacco has drawn only part of each illustration in color?

6. **Connecting/Comparing** How does this story help you understand traditions and what they mean to families?

Narrating

Write a Story

You know how Patricia Polacco feels about the Keeping Quilt. How would the quilt's story be different if the quilt were telling it? What parts would be the same? Write the quilt's version of the Polacco family history.

Tips
- Make a story map to help you remember people and events.
- Look closely at the illustrations for ideas.

Social Studies

Make a Family Tree

Draw the Polacco family tree. At the top of it, write the names of the oldest family members. List husbands and wives beside each other. Then write children's names below their parents. Draw lines to connect relatives. Look back at the story as you work.

Art

Make a Class Keeping Quilt

Celebrate the year with a paper Keeping Quilt. Create a quilt square that shows a favorite event, person, or place. Then make a class quilt from the squares. You can add to it all year long.

Internet

Complete a Web Crossword Puzzle

Take a vocabulary challenge! Print a crossword puzzle about *The Keeping Quilt* from Education Place.

www.eduplace.com/kids

Skill: How to Take Notes

1. Write the **title** at the top of a piece of paper.

2. Look for **main ideas** as you read.

3. Write a **heading** for each main idea. Use key words or phrases.

4. List important **details** below each heading.

5. Read your notes to make sure that they make sense.

Nesting Dolls

by Marie E. Kingdon

Have you ever seen a nesting or stacking doll? A nesting doll is brightly painted, made of wood, and opens into two parts — a top and a bottom.

Do you know why they are called "nesting" dolls? When you open the first doll, there's another doll nested inside. Sometimes there are two or three dolls inside. Sometimes there are five or even ten or more. Guess how many are in the largest nesting doll we know about in the world? Would you believe, seventy-two! The largest doll in that set is three feet tall.

When you open each doll, there's another doll nested inside.

154

Some of the first nesting dolls were made in China a very, very long time ago — some say even a thousand years. Today nesting dolls are made in Poland, China, the Netherlands, India, and even the United States of America. But the best and the prettiest are made in Russia, where they are called "Matryoshkas" [maht-ree-OSH-kahs]. This comes from a common name for women in Russian country villages, "Mastryona," [mahst-ree-OH-nah] or village mother. Nesting, or Matryoshka, dolls are often given as gifts to new babies in Russia.

Some nesting dolls have a whole family inside: father, mother, sister, brother. Some Matryoshkas open and have ten solid dolls, all the same size, inside. These are called "counting Matryoshkas" because they help Russian children learn to count.

Here is a family of nesting dolls.

Matryoshka dolls made in Russia come from different regions, just as different products come from different states in America. Nesting, or Matryoshka, dolls are hand-painted and are dressed in costumes from the region where they are made. Some wear aprons and kerchiefs or scarves. Some hold flowers or baskets. The most common dolls are brightly painted in reds and yellows and have many coats of lacquer to protect them. Other dolls are painted in greens, blues, pastels, and even gold metallic.

A very fine set of dolls from Russia might have a different scene from a fairy tale on each doll in the series. These dolls tell a story with pictures, not words.

Nesting dolls are pretty, and they are great for play. Some children even have collections of different nesting dolls. These dolls can be fun for everyone. Tell your friends what you have learned about Matryoshkas. Have fun looking at and playing with these interesting, unique, wooden dolls.

Instructions

The purpose of writing instructions is to tell others how to do or make something. Use this student's writing as a model when you write instructions of your own.

Titles for instructions usually tell what the writing is about.

How to Have a Great Thanksgiving

My favorite celebration is on Thanksgiving.

I really like Thanksgiving because of all the stuff

that we do together. If you want to have a great

Thanksgiving like mine, here's how to do it.

First, wake up in the morning and take a

deep breath. Smell the turkey cooking and the

sweet potatoes baking.

Then go downstairs to the living room and

watch the Thanksgiving parade on TV. Look for all

Topic sentences make a good **beginning** for a piece of writing.

158

the GREAT floats and BIG balloons. You'll really like it. I wait all year just to watch the parade.

After that, it's the afternoon. You should invite your whole family over to enjoy the tasty dinner. Everyone at our house eats, talks, and then watches the football game.

If you follow these steps, you will have a great Thanksgiving just like mine.

Meet the Author

Jamie S.

Grade: three
State: New York
Hobbies: playing school
What she'd like to be when she grows up: a teacher

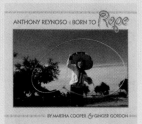

Riding and Roping

Long ago, much of the southwestern United States was part of Mexico. Today, Mexican customs and traditions are still celebrated in the Southwest. One of these traditions is Mexico's national sport, the **rodeo**. At a rodeo, cowboys called *charros* show off their roping and riding skills.

A rodeo isn't the only place to enjoy Mexican American traditions. **Performers** often get together at an **exhibition** to share their riding, dancing, or roping talents with others. In the next selection, a boy from Arizona tells you about his talents and traditions — and how he celebrates them every day.

These *charras* ▶ (cowgirls) worked hard to become **experts** at riding as a team.

160

◀ A talented charro often becomes a **celebrity** just like other sports stars.

▼ Arizona is located in the southwestern part of the United States.

161

ANTHONY REYNOSO ⸱ BORN TO Rope

BY MARTHA COOPER & GINGER GORDON

Strategy Focus

As you read about Anthony Reynoso, think of **questions** about his family and their traditions that you would like to discuss later.

$\mathcal{M}$y name is Anthony Reynoso. I'm named after my father, who is holding the white horse, and my grandfather, who is holding the dappled horse. We all rope and ride Mexican Rodeo style on my grandfather's ranch outside of Phoenix, Arizona.

As soon as I could stand, my dad gave me a rope. I had my own little hat and everything else I needed to dress as a *charro*. That's what a Mexican cowboy is called. It's a good thing I started when I was little, because it takes years to learn to rope.

I live with my mom and dad in the little Mexican-American and Yaqui Indian town of Guadalupe. All my grandparents live close by. This will help a lot when the new baby comes. My mom is pregnant.

I've got a secret about Guadalupe. I know where there are petroglyphs in the rocks right near my house. My favorite looks like a man with a shield. People carved these petroglyphs hundreds of years ago. Why did they do it? I wonder what the carvings mean.

Every Sunday morning the old Mexican Mission church is packed. At Easter, lots of people come to watch the Yaqui Indian ceremonies in the center of town. No one's allowed to take photographs, but an artist painted this wall showing the Yaqui dancers.

Some Sundays, we go to Casa Reynoso, my grandparents' restaurant. If it's very busy, my cousins and I pitch in. When there's time, my grandmother lets me help in the kitchen. Casa Reynoso has the best Mexican food in town.

On holidays, we go to my grandfather's ranch. Once a year, we all get dressed up for a family photo.

I've got lots of cousins. Whenever there's a
birthday we have a piñata. We smash it with
a stick until all the candy falls out. Then we
scramble to grab as much as we can hold.

Best of all, at the ranch we get to practice roping on horseback. My dad's always trying something new . . . and so am I!

In Mexico, the Rodeo is the national sport. The most famous charros there are like sports stars here.

On weekdays, Dad runs his landscape business, Mom works in a public school, and I go to school. I wait for the bus with other kids at the corner of my block.

I always come to school with my homework done. When I'm in class, I forget about roping and riding. I don't think anyone in school knows about it except my best friends.

It's different when I get home. I practice hard with Dad. He's a good teacher and shows me everything his father taught him. We spend a lot of time practicing for shows at schools, malls, and rodeos. We are experts at passing the rope. Our next big exhibition is in Sedona, about two hours away by car.

After rope practice we shoot a few baskets. Dad's pretty good at that too!

On Friday after school, Dad and I prepare our ropes for the show in Sedona. They've got to be just right.

Everything's ready for tomorrow, so I can take a break and go through my basketball cards. I decide which ones I want to buy, sell, and trade. Collecting basketball cards is one of my favorite hobbies.

It's Saturday! Time for the show in Sedona. I get a little nervous watching the other performers. I sure wouldn't want to get messed up in my own rope in front of all these people! After the Mexican hat dance, we're next!

My dad goes first . . . and then it's my turn. While the mariachis play, I do my stuff. Even Dad can't spin the rope from his teeth like this!

Then Dad and I rope together, just like we practiced.
It's hard to do with our wide charro hats on. When my
dad passes the rope to me and I spin it well, he says he has
passed the Mexican Rodeo tradition on to me. Now it's up
to me to keep it going.

Mom is our best fan. She always comes with us.
It makes me feel good to know she's out there watching.

Sometimes tourists want us to pose for pictures with them. It makes me feel like a celebrity.

After the show, boy, are we hungry! We pack up and eat a quick lunch. Then we go to a special place called Slide Rock.

Slide Rock is a natural water slide where kids have played for hundreds, maybe even thousands, of years. It's cold today! I'd rather come back in the summer when it's hot. But Dad pulls me in anyway. Brrr!

Time to go home. Next time we come to Sedona, the baby will be with us. I wonder if it will be a boy or a girl. It's hard to wait!

I'm going to love being a big brother. Pretty soon the baby will be wearing my old boots and learning how to rope from me.

Meet the Author
Ginger Gordon

Ginger Gordon teaches at a school in New York City. Gordon's first children's book, *My Two Worlds,* was about one of her students, Kirsy Rodriguez. Kirsy inspired Gordon with her energy and sense of adventure — just as Anthony Reynoso did.

Meet the Photographer
Martha Cooper

It's good that Martha Cooper lives in New York City, because it is one of her favorite places to photograph. Her photos show many different sides of city life, from subway art to Chinese New Year celebrations. She also worked with Ginger Gordon on *My Two Worlds.*

Other books:

The Marble Book (by Richie Chevat)
Lion Dancer: Ernie Wan's Chinese New Year (by Kate Waters)
The Jump Rope Book (by Elizabeth Loredo)

Visit Education Place and discover more about Ginger Gordon and Martha Cooper. **www.eduplace.com/kids**

Think About the Selection

1. Why does Anthony work so hard at roping? What activities do *you* work hard at?

2. Why doesn't Anthony think or talk about roping when he is in school?

3. How does Anthony's whole family help to celebrate the roping tradition?

4. Why will it be important for Anthony to teach the roping tradition to the new baby?

5. Which of Anthony's activities would you describe as traditions? Explain your answer.

6. **Connecting/Comparing** Both this story and *The Keeping Quilt* tell about sharing traditions. How are these traditions the same and different?

Write a Comparison

Make a list of Anthony's hobbies and interests. Then make a list of your own hobbies and interests. In a paragraph, explain how your interests and Anthony's are different and how they are the same. Then tell which of Anthony's activities you'd like to try.

Tips

- Reread the parts of the story that describe what Anthony likes.
- Make a Venn diagram to sort the activities.

Draw Yourself as an Expert

What activity are you an expert at? It might be practicing a musical instrument, playing a sport, or doing a science experiment. Draw a picture of yourself that shows your special talent. Label the things you use in your activity.

Make an Announcement

At a rodeo, an announcer introduces each event. With a partner, take turns role-playing what the announcer introducing Anthony Reynoso might say. Include who and what the audience will be seeing.

Tips

- Begin with "Ladies and gentlemen. . . ."
- Use expression to get the audience's attention.

Internet

Complete a Web Word Find

Pick up a pencil and rope some words you've learned in the story! Print a word-find puzzle from Education Place.

www.eduplace.com/kids

Spotlight

CHRIS COLWILL, 10

Talent with a Twist

by
Pat
Robbins

Chris Colwill has just taken a flying leap off a diving board. He focuses on the sky, then on the water, so he'll know when to kick out of his full twisting one-and-a-half dive and slice the water hands first. At nine Chris became the youngest member of the United States Junior Olympic national team, earning two gold medals and a bronze at his first international meet.

Chris, who is hearing impaired, lives in Brandon, Florida. He practices daily with a coach, reading the coach's lips after each dive for tips on how to improve. "I don't mind working hard," Chris says. "I like to do my best."

All That Jazz

by
Judith E.
Rinard

JAMIE KNIGHT, 10

When jazz singer Jamie Knight steps on stage, she doesn't miss a beat. At nine, Jamie performed at New York's Carnegie Hall. She brought down the house with her version of jazz classics such as "It Don't Mean a Thing If It Ain't Got That Swing." "I try my very best to put the audience into the music with me," says the pint-size performer from Philadelphia, Pennsylvania.

Jamie has sung at jazz festivals, appeared on TV's *Good Morning America*, and released her own CD. A performer since age six, she likes all kinds of music but says, "Jazz is different. It has its own flavor."

183

Flamenco Fantástico

by
Jane R.
McGoldrick

ELENA CHAVEZ, 10

She spins. She stomps. Sharply, smartly, she tosses a glance over one shoulder, then the other. This is Elena Chavez. And this is flamenco [fluh-MEHN-koh], a traditional dance style that started in southern Spain. Elena performs in the grand finale of a flamenco show every evening in her hometown of Granada, in Spain. She has appeared on television and has won international prizes for her dancing talent. She matches fancy footwork and flowing arm movements to the pulsing rhythm of guitars or violins. "In flamenco, you feel the music and express it in movement," says Elena.

Musical Maestros... Relatively Speaking

by
Minna
Morse

THE CHOI FAMILY

The Choi family of Calgary, Alberta, in Canada, is a family that plays together and stays together. They are gifted musicians who practice for several hours nearly every day. "When we practice together, it gets really noisy," says Rosabel, on the piano.

Each child learned to play the piano first, then other instruments. Rosabel, eighteen, plays the flute. She has won national competitions in Canada and even performed with the Calgary Philharmonic Orchestra.

Edward, fourteen, plays the clarinet. He plans a career in music. The two youngest Chois — Arnold, nine, and Estelle, eight — play the cello. Both have won national music awards.

Playing as well as the Chois do takes practice and dedication as well as talent. "You have to sacrifice a lot of time," says Rosabel, "but I give myself one day a week to do other things." What makes the Chois practice so much? "It's just a love of music," says Edward.

THE
TALKING
CLOTH

STORY AND
PICTURES BY
Rhonda
Mitchell

Background and Vocabulary

Handmade Cloth from Ghana

The Ashanti are a group of people from Ghana, a country in West Africa. The Ashanti make a beautiful kind of cloth called adinkra cloth. In the past, adinkra cloth was very expensive. Having an adinkra cloth was a sign of **wealth**. **Royalty**, such as kings and queens, often wore it. But today, the markets of Ghana are filled with adinkra cloth.

◄ **Adinkra cloth is a beautiful way to remember the past, and the Ashanti people are proud to wear it.**

One store in a market might have a collection of many different cloths.

Parts of the adinkra cloth have colorful, embroidered patterns. Other parts are stamped with symbols. Each symbol has a different meaning. In the next story, you will learn how these symbols often tell something about the person who wears the cloth.

Europe

Asia

Africa

Ghana

Atlantic Ocean

187

Meet the
AUTHOR AND ILLUSTRATOR

Rhonda Mitchell

Birthday: February 22

Where she was born: Cleveland, Ohio

How she became a children's book illustrator:
Mitchell has always enjoyed painting pictures of people. One day, a children's author named Angela Johnson asked Mitchell to paint pictures for some of her books. Mitchell did, and she loved it!

Why "The Talking Cloth" is important to her:
Mitchell liked illustrating children's books so much that she decided to write one of her own. *The Talking Cloth* is the first book she has written. And, of course, she also painted the pictures.

Some other things she likes:
Cats, tennis, living in a small town

Find out more about Rhonda Mitchell by visiting Education Place. **www.eduplace.com/kids**

188

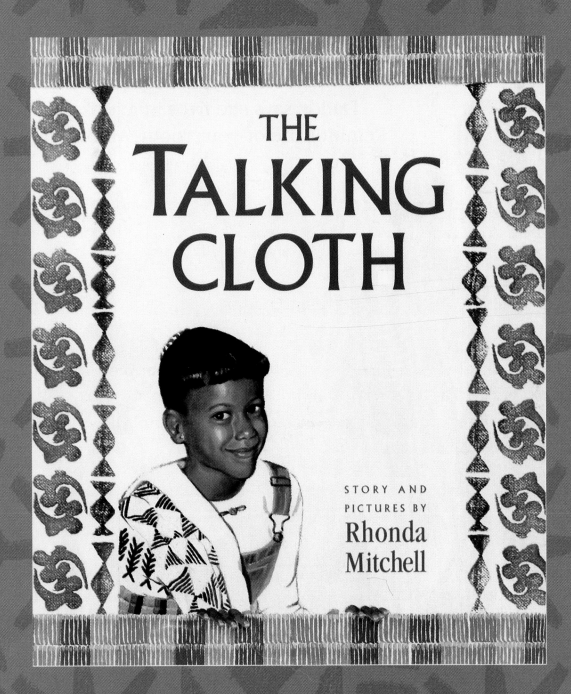

THE TALKING CLOTH

STORY AND PICTURES BY
Rhonda Mitchell

Strategy Focus

As you read, **summarize** what the Talking Cloth means to Amber and her family.

189

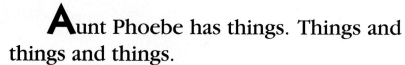

Aunt Phoebe has things. Things and things and things.

"A collector of life," Mom calls her.

Daddy says she lives in a junk pile.

"Reminds me of your room, Amber," he says.

I like visiting Aunt Phoebe. There's no place in her house to be bored, and she always gives me mocha to drink. Daddy says it will stunt my growth.

Aunt Phoebe tells him, "Mocha is named after a city in Yemen, and this child just grew an inch or two, *inside*, for knowing that."

Aunt Phoebe knows things. . . .

She tells me stories, about her "collection of life," each time we visit. I sip hot mocha and listen, imagining all the people and places she has seen.

Today we sit in her kitchen and she tells about the basket of folded cloths in the corner. "I bought these in Africa," she says.

Daddy laughs. "I figured that was laundry you hadn't put away."

Aunt Phoebe smiles and takes a cloth from the top of the basket. She unfolds it with a flourish — a long magic carpet. It runs like a white river across the floor.

"What do you do with such a long cloth?" I ask.

"You wear it," says Aunt Phoebe. "It tells how you are feeling. This cloth talks."

"How can it do that?"

"By its color and what the symbols mean," Aunt Phoebe tells me. "This is *adinkra* cloth from Ghana. It's made by the Ashanti people and at one time only royalty wore it," she says.

Aunt Phoebe rubs the cloth against my face. It's silk and feels smooth. I imagine myself an Ashanti princess. . . .

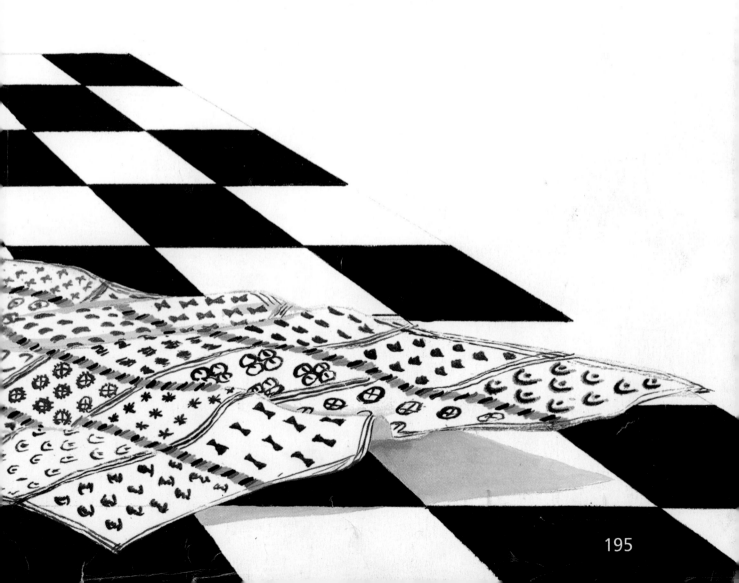

The cloth is embroidered in sections and hand printed all over with small black symbols. Like words.

A white cloth means joy — yellow, gold or riches. Green stands for newness and growth. Blue is a sign of love, but red is worn only for sad times, like funerals or during wars.

"Maybe I should wear red when your daddy comes to visit," Aunt Phoebe says.

Daddy laughs and pours himself some mocha. He likes to listen too. I know it.

Aunt Phoebe tells the meaning of some symbols on her cloth. One says, "Except God I fear none." That's called *Gye Nyame*.

Another is called *Obi nka Obie*. "I offend no one without cause."

Each symbol speaks of something different, like faith, power, or love.

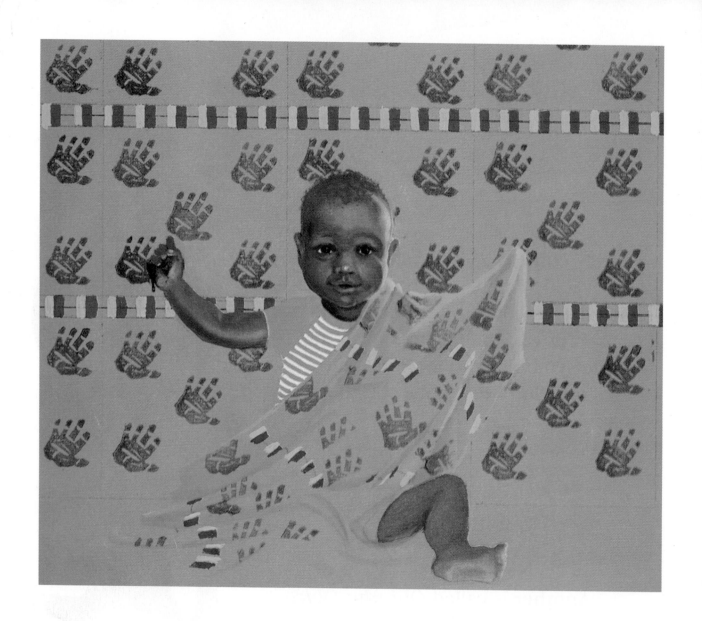

I imagine cloths with my own symbols on them.

Fred — he's my little brother — should be dressed
in green for "go" with grubby little handprints all over.
Everyone can see what kind of a mess that kid is.

Aunt Phoebe's little brother is my daddy. "Let's see,"
she says. "Guess we could wrap him in gray pinstripe
cloth for seriousness, with squares on it!"

We all laugh, imagining that.

I ask if I can put on the *adinkra* cloth.

"Of course you can, baby," Aunt Phoebe says. "When you're older, you can have it for your own."

She wraps the *adinkra* three times around my waist, then across one shoulder — and still it drags on the ground.

"A cloth this long is a sign of wealth," she tells me.

Daddy says, "Amber, you'll need to drink a lot of mocha to grow tall enough."

"Well," says Aunt Phoebe, "this child has grown a lot, *inside*, just today!"

I smile, thinking of it. This cloth means joy.

I am an Ashanti princess now, and here is all my family and everyone who has ever worn an *adinkra* . . .

gathered around me.

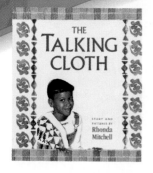

Think About the Selection

1. Why do you think Aunt Phoebe likes to collect things?

2. Why does Amber enjoy visiting Aunt Phoebe? Would you like to visit Aunt Phoebe? Explain your answer.

3. How does the Talking Cloth "talk," and what does the cloth say?

4. What does Aunt Phoebe mean when she says that Amber has grown *inside*?

5. If you had an adinkra cloth, what would it look like? What would your cloth say about you?

6. **Connecting/Comparing** How is the Keeping Quilt also a kind of Talking Cloth?

Describing

Write a Character Sketch

Describe your favorite character in the story. Use facts from the story to help you guess the character's favorite activities, items, foods, and clothes. Include adjectives such as *serious* or *adventurous* to describe how the character acts.

Tips

- **To get started, create a word web about the character.**
- **Put the most important details at the beginning of your sketch.**

Write Number Sentences

Look carefully at pages 194–195. How many squares do you see in the Talking Cloth? Write number sentences to describe the total number of squares. Try to write at least four different sentences.

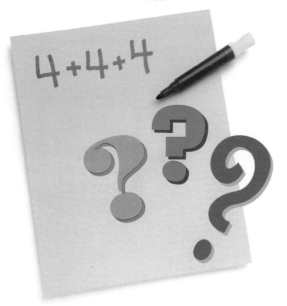

Make Symbol Flashcards

Find five symbols in your classroom, neighborhood, or home. Draw each symbol on a different card. On the back of each card, write what the symbol means. Then ask a classmate to guess the meaning of each symbol.

Bonus Create a symbol that says something about you. Ask your partner to guess what it means.

Internet

E-mail a Friend

Amber's Aunt Phoebe likes to collect things. Do you think collecting is fun? Do you have a collection now? What might you like to collect? Send an e-mail and tell a friend what you think.

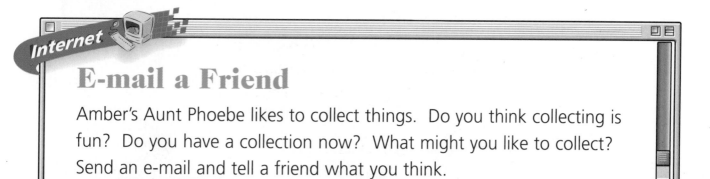

A Healthy Recipe from Ghana

by Deanna F. Cook

In Ghana, peanuts are called groundnuts because they grow underground. Ghanians eat groundnuts — a big source of protein — almost every day. To make peanut butter, they mash groundnuts using a mortar and pestle. If you have a food processor, this is a faster way to make it.

My Peanut Butter

Homemade Peanut Butter

2 cups (500 ml) unsalted roasted peanuts

1 tablespoon (15 ml) vegetable oil

Here's What You Do

1 Pour the shelled peanuts and vegetable oil into the bowl of a food processor.

2 With the help of a grown-up, process the peanuts for about 3 minutes, or until smooth.

Makes 1 cup (250 ml) of all-natural, creamy peanut butter. Put any leftovers in the refrigerator.

Dancing Rainbows

NATIVE AMERICAN DANCE

Dance has always been an important part of many Native American cultures. Native American children often learn to dance by **imitating** older members of their family or community. The **elders** may teach children different traditional dances that have been performed for a long time.

These dances can have many meanings. In some dances, Native Americans show **respect** for their **ancestors** who have lived before them. In others, they **honor** the sun and the earth.

Through their traditional dances, Native Americans remember their past and share their memories and history with each other. Dancing is one way they celebrate their lives.

This Native American dancer wears a traditional costume as she performs.

Young Native Americans, such as the boy in the next selection, may enjoy performing and watching traditional dances.

Meet the
Author and Photographer
Evelyn Clarke Mott

Fact File

▶ Mott was born on August 22 in Portchester, New York.

▶ At the age of ten, Mott won three dollars in a newspaper's writing contest.

▶ For her book *Balloon Ride*, Mott had to ride in a hot-air balloon. There was only one problem — she was afraid of high places! At first, it was hard to take pictures because her hands and legs were shaking. After a while, she lost her fear and finished the book.

▶ Mott also likes music, art, hiking, traveling, and looking at the stars.

You can learn more about Evelyn Clarke Mott by visiting Education Place. **www.eduplace.com/kids**

DANCING RAINBOWS

A Pueblo Boy's Story

Evelyn Clarke Mott

How are dancing, rain, and rainbows important to Curt and his family? As you read, **monitor** your understanding. Reread to **clarify** anything that's confusing.

It is the day before Feast Day. Curt and his grandpa, Andy, are excited. Every year, on June 24, their pueblo has a big party with food, fun, and dance.

Pueblo is a Spanish word for town. Curt and Andy Garcia are Pueblo Indians. Their tribe is called Tewa. They live in San Juan Pueblo, New Mexico.

210

San Juan Pueblo is named after Saint John. On Feast Day, native dances honor the pueblo's patron saint and celebrate the power of the summer sun.

Curt's ancestors were farmers. They grew corn, beans, and squash. Now most Tewas work at businesses outside the pueblo, but some still farm.

"We must always take care of our land," Andy tells Curt. "We must respect Mother Earth."

Curt spends a lot of time with his grandpa. He learns so much. They share many laughs.

Andy is an elder in his tribe. That means he is very respected. He is well known among his people as a great dancer. "Dance with all your heart!" Andy says.

All Tewa dances are prayers. The Tewa people dance
to cure the sick, to give thanks, to bring the tribe together,
to pray for good crops, and to have fun! Because the
Tewas' land is very dry, every dance is also a prayer
for rain.

"Let's hurry, Grandpa!" Curt says. "It's time for the
Buffalo Dance!" Curt and Andy rush to the plaza.

The plaza is the center of town. It is where the tribe meets.
Three people dance in buffalo costume.

Tewas believe that people and animals once spoke the same
language. This ended when people started to lose respect for the
animals. Tewas show their respect for all animals with the Buffalo
Dance. This dance blesses tomorrow's Feast Day. It is said to give
the tribe strength and power.

The smell of baking bread welcomes Curt and Andy home from the dance. For Feast Day, Curt's mom and relatives all help bake over seventy loaves of bread in the horno, an oven for baking bread, cakes, and cookies. It is shaped like a beehive.

The horno sits outside the house. Curt's mom makes a fire to heat up the oven. Then she cleans out the ashes and puts in the dough.

The dough bakes in the warm oven. Curt's mom pulls out the hot bread. Dogs wait near the horno eager for a taste!

The Garcia house smells of stew, bread, cakes, and candy. Everyone looks forward to tomorrow's feast!

Andy wakes up early on Feast Day. He prays in the hills. He asks for a good mind, a good heart, and a good life. He sprinkles some cornmeal as a gift to the earth.

Today looks bright and sunny. But even if it rains, everyone will dance. Tewas believe rain is good luck. They say their ancestors come back as raindrops to help them live.

Rainbows are also good luck. They join Mother Earth with Father Sky.

Soon all the Garcias are awake. Everyone hurries to get ready. Andy's wife, Verna, sprinkles salt on his head. She says it keeps away bad spirits.

Andy helps Curt put on face paint. Curt pulls a fox skin over his head. He puts on his Comanche costume.

Andy fixes his bustle. He ties on his headdress. With everyone ready, the Garcias head toward the plaza.

BOOM! BOOM! BOOM! The drummers move through the crowd.

Indians say drums have great power. They believe a drum sounds the heartbeat of Mother Earth. Drummers paint their hands white to give their drumbeats more power.

The drummers sing in Tewa. They sing of many things. Plants. Animals. Clouds. Rainbows. They try to sing like birds. Bird songs are so beautiful.

The Comanche Dance starts. Over a hundred Tewas, from three to eighty years old, move their feet to the beat of the drum.

In this dance, they are imitating the Comanche warriors, acting as they would in battle. The dancers pray for the Tewa tribe and give thanks for their blessings.

Colors twirl
and swirl.

Andy dances proudly.

Tewas dance their thanks to the Great Spirit. They pray for their tribe's happiness. They pray for Mother Earth.

Jingle . . . Jingle . . . Jingle. Bells ring as Curt moves his feet. He thinks of his grandpa's words, "A Tewa never dances for himself. He dances for all things and people." Curt sends out prayers to the crowd. He wishes them a good life and a safe trip home.

In 1923, the United States made Indian worship illegal. Tewas could no longer visit their kivas — a place of worship. Indians could not dance. All Indian dances were seen as war dances. It wasn't until 1934 that Indians could dance again.

Now, at Feast Day, the flag flies proudly. Many Tewas have fought for their country. Some dancers show pride for their country.

Tewa women dance with grace. To celebrate the power of the sun, they paint the red sun on their cheeks.

The men yelp loudly for the Comanche Dance. They wear fancy costumes.

Tewa children dance with honor. They learn to dance as soon as they walk. That is why they are good, strong dancers.

Costumes have many meanings. Shells sound like waves hitting the shore. Tassels look like raindrops. Bells sound like falling rain. Embroidered designs look like clouds.

The dancers go home for the feast. Tewa homes fill with friends and family. There is so much to eat. Andy says he doesn't hear any talking. Only chewing!

After the feast, everyone meets at the plaza. They dance again in the hot sun. As the sun sets, the dancers go home.

Sometimes, Curt and Andy practice their dances. Andy teaches Curt. Curt respects his grandpa because he is very wise. Curt tries to be like his grandpa.

Curt and his brothers do the Eagle Dance. They swoop, soar, land, circle, and rest. They keep perfect time to the beat of the drum.

The eagle flies higher than any other bird. Tewas believe that eagles are messengers. They say that eagles bring prayers to the clouds and messages back to the earth. Tewas dance to give thanks to the great bird.

Andy started a dance group for Curt and other young Tewa dancers. The group often dances outside the pueblo. Fairs. Schools. Hospitals. Powwows.

The day after Feast Day, Curt dances at a city fair. He says it doesn't matter where he dances. His prayers still reach the clouds.

Curt is proud to be Tewa. His ancestors have given him so much. Beautiful songs. Colorful dances. Curt is happy to follow his grandpa's footsteps. Dancing for rain. And rainbows.

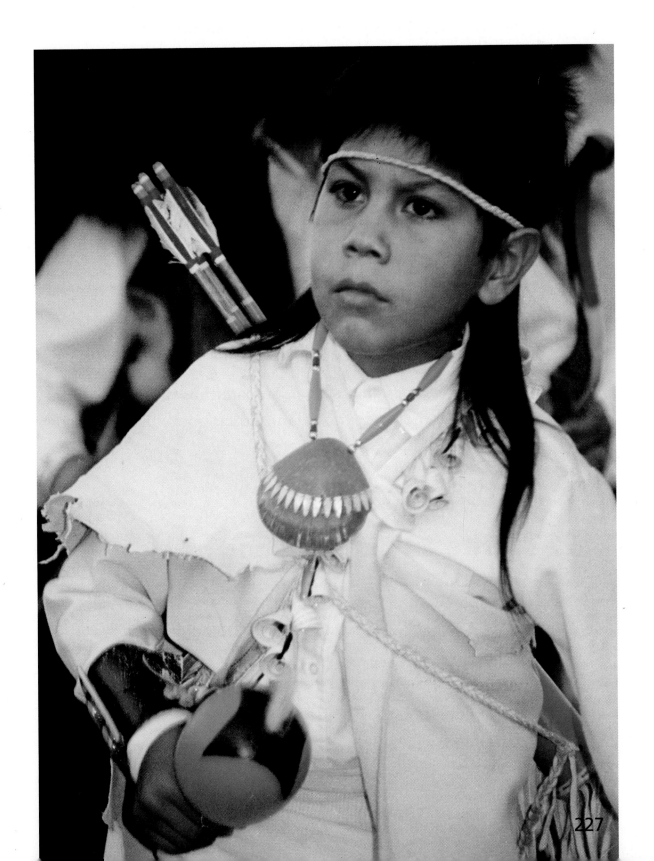

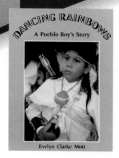

Think About the Selection

1. Why do you think Curt respects his grandpa and tries to be like him?

2. Why do you think Andy started a dance group for young Tewas?

3. How does Curt follow Andy's advice to "dance with all your heart"? What do *you* do with all your heart?

4. What does Andy mean when he says, "A Tewa never dances for himself. He dances for all things and people"?

5. How does Andy teach younger family members about the past? What are some ways *you* learn about the past?

6. **Connecting/Comparing** Compare the ways both Curt and Anthony Reynoso honor their ancestors and share their traditions.

Explaining

Write an Explanation

How do Curt and his family prepare for the Feast Day? Write an explanation that tells what each person does to get ready for the celebration.

> **Tips**
>
> - To begin, go back to the selection and take notes.
> - Organize your explanation by topic, main ideas, and supporting details.

Link Geography to Your Community

In a small group, look at the big photograph on pages 216–217. Describe the land and climate where Curt and Andy live. Discuss how their surroundings affect life in their community. Then discuss how your surroundings affect life in your own community.

Draw the Water Cycle

Where does rain come from, and where does it go? Draw a diagram explaining the water cycle. Include the earth, water, sun, air, clouds, and rain. Use arrows to show the path of the water. Label each part of the cycle. Use an encyclopedia or a science book for information.

Bonus Show how the water cycle changes at different times of the year.

Internet

Send an E-postcard

Choose one of the traditions you have discovered in this theme. Send a friend an E-postcard telling him or her all about it. You'll find one at Education Place. **www.eduplace.com/kids**

Rain and Rainbows

by Neil Ardley

Why does a dazzling arch of color form when the sun lights up a rain shower? Find out by adding a little sunshine to a bowl of water.

Skill: How to Follow Directions

❶ **Read** all of the directions carefully.

❷ **Gather** the items you'll need.

❸ **Look at** the pictures to help you understand.

❹ **Follow** the steps in the correct order.

❺ **Reread** each step as you work.

Did You Know?

You can see a rainbow in a rain shower if the sun is behind you. Each raindrop is a round mass of water that splits the sunlight into different colors and reflects them back at you.

Making a Rainbow

You will need:

Fishbowl filled with water **Black cardboard** **White cardboard**

1. Move a table to a sunny place. Lay the black cardboard on the table, then set the fishbowl on top.

2. Hold the white cardboard off to one side of the fishbowl. Hold it so that the side of the cardboard facing you is shaded. A rainbow appears on the cardboard!

As the sunlight passes through the round mass of water, it splits into the colors of the rainbow, which are reflected onto the cardboard.

231

Filling in the Blank

Some test items ask you to complete a sentence. You will have three or four answers to choose from. How do you choose the best answer? Look at this sample test item for *Dancing Rainbows*. The correct answer is shown. Use the tips to help you answer this kind of test item.

Tips

- Read the directions carefully.
- Read the sentence to yourself by using each answer choice to fill in the blank.
- Look back at the selection if you need to.
- Fill in the answer circle completely.
- After you finish a test, check your answers if you have time.

Read the sentence. At the bottom of the page, fill in the circle for the answer that best completes the sentence.

1 **Curt spends a lot of time with Andy because —**

Ⓐ Andy is an elder in the tribe.

Ⓑ Curt likes wearing costumes.

Ⓒ Curt learns so much from him.

Ⓓ Andy started a dance group.

ANSWER ROW 1   Ⓐ Ⓑ ● Ⓓ

232

Now see how one student figured out the best answer.

Trickster Tales

TRICKSTER TALES are a kind of folktale. Clever characters and plenty of mischief make these tales popular in cultures all over the world.

In a trickster tale . . .

- a clever animal or person plays a trick on other characters;
- the trickster character has one or two main qualities, such as greediness or boastfulness;
- the language sounds as if someone were telling the tale out loud.

Contents

Hungry Spider

A Tale from Africa (Ashanti Tribe)

told by Pleasant DeSpain
illustrated by Daniel Moreton

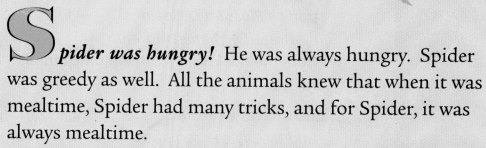

S*pider was hungry!* He was always hungry. Spider was greedy as well. All the animals knew that when it was mealtime, Spider had many tricks, and for Spider, it was always mealtime.

One day Turtle left his home in the pond and went on a long journey. He traveled slowly through the jungle and finally arrived at Spider's house. They had never met each other before this, and Spider reluctantly invited Turtle to stay for dinner. Spider liked to talk to strangers, as they had interesting stories to tell. But he hated to feed them because they ate food that he wanted for himself.

"Friend Turtle," said Spider, "you must be tired after your long trip. Go down to the river and refresh yourself. I'll prepare our dinner while you are gone."

"How kind of you," said Turtle. "I'll hurry as I'm quite hungry." Turtle followed the trail to the water's edge and scrambled in. It was good to cool down and feel clean again. He crawled out of the river and hurried back to Spider's house. Delicious odors filled the air. It was time to eat!

Turtle walked in and saw the food on the table. "Thank you for inviting me to stay for dinner, Spider," said Turtle. "I haven't eaten all day."

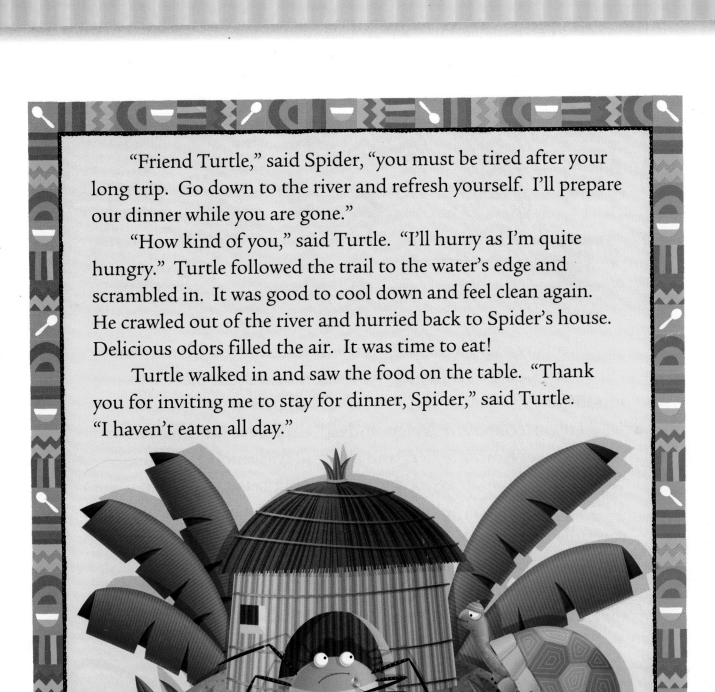

"You are most welcome, Turtle," said Spider with a frown. "But in this part of the country, we don't sit at the table with muddy feet."

Turtle looked at his feet. Indeed, they were muddy. His feet were wet from the river and the trail was thick with dust. He was most embarrassed. He excused himself and walked all the way back to the river to wash them off. He dried them carefully on the grass and hurried back to Spider. But he was too late. Spider had eaten all the food. Turtle was disappointed, but too polite to complain. He slept hungry that night and left for home in the morning even hungrier!

everal months later, Spider went on a long journey. He arrived at Turtle's house and asked if he could spend the night.

"Of course, friend Spider," said Turtle. "I remember how good you were to me."

"I'm famished!" exclaimed Spider. "Could we eat right away?"

"I'll dive to the bottom of the pond and prepare a feast," said Turtle. "Wait here and I'll call you when all is ready."

Turtle gathered his best-tasting food and set it on a long table at the bottom of the pond. Then he swam to the surface and said, "Please join me, Spider. Dinner is served."

Spider leaped into the water and tried to dive down. But he weighed so little that he couldn't stay underwater, let alone sink to the bottom. Turtle had already started to eat, so Spider kicked and jerked and splashed with all of his strength. And he stayed right on top.

Turtle swam to the surface and said, "Friend Spider, come down and enjoy the meal. It's quite good, if I do say so."

Spider had an idea! He scrambled back to shore and picked up several heavy pebbles. He stuffed them in his coat pockets to weigh him down. Spider then hopped back into the pond and sank quickly to the bottom. The food was half gone, but what was left looked delicious! He had started to take a big bite when Turtle said, "Friend Spider, in this part of the jungle, it's considered bad manners to eat with your coat on."

Spider didn't want to be impolite. So he slipped out of his coat and reached for another morsel of food. But before he could grab hold of it, he bobbed to the surface like a cork! Spider cried as he floated about, watching Turtle down on the bottom of the pond eating the rest of the food.

It is said that one kindness deserves another.

Rabbit Races with Turtle

told by Gayle Ross
illustrated by Murv Jacob

It is true that Rabbit loved to brag and exaggerate about all the things he could do, but one thing that everyone agreed on was that he was a very fast runner. Turtle loved to boast too, however, and one day he told the people that he was even faster than Rabbit. Rabbit heard about Turtle's claim, and they

began to argue so fiercely that everyone agreed the only way to settle the matter was to have a race between the two. It was decided that Turtle and Rabbit would race over four mountain ridges, and the one who came over the fourth ridge first would be the winner.

Now, no one had ever seen Turtle move at anything but the slowest of paces, so Rabbit was certain of his ability to win. So sure was he that he told Turtle, "You know you can't run. You could never win a race with me. I will give you the first ridge. You will have to cross only three, while I cross all four."

Turtle agreed to Rabbit's terms, but that night he called together all his turtle relatives. "You must help me put an end to Rabbit's boasting," said Turtle. He explained his plan to his family, and they all agreed to help.

When the day of the race came, all the animals gathered. Some came to the starting point to see the runners off. Others waited on the fourth ridge to declare the winner. Rabbit came to the starting point, but Turtle had gone ahead to the next ridge as Rabbit had arranged. The others could just see his shiny back through the long grass. The signal was given, and the race began!

Rabbit burst from the starting point with his long jumps, expecting to win the race before Turtle could even make it down his first ridge. Imagine his surprise when he came to the top of the ridge and saw Turtle disappearing over the top of the next mountain!

Rabbit ran even faster, and when he came to the top of the second mountain, he looked all around, expecting to see Turtle somewhere in the long grass. He looked up — and there was the sun glinting off Turtle's shell as he crossed the third ridge!

Now Rabbit was truly surprised, and he was beginning to be worried. He gave his longest jumps ever to catch up. When he reached the top of the third ridge, he was so tired and out of breath he could only fall over and cry as he watched Turtle cross the fourth mountain and win the race!

The other animals gave the race to Turtle, and everyone wondered how slow Turtle had managed to beat Rabbit. Turtle just smiled and never spoke of it, but it was really very easy.

All Turtle's relatives look just alike, so Turtle had placed one near the top of each ridge. Whenever Rabbit had come into sight, a Turtle relative had crawled to the top of the mountain ahead of him and then hidden in the tall grass. Turtle himself had climbed the fourth ridge to cross the finish line.

So Turtle won the race with a very good trick of his own. But if he had hoped to stop Rabbit's bragging, he was surely disappointed. No one has ever been able to do that.

Aunt Fox and the Fried Fish

told by Rafael Rivero Oramas
illustrated by Richard Bernal

Early one morning, Uncle Fox was strolling through the forest when he came upon a river full of fish. Watching the fish jump and splash made Uncle Fox very hungry, so he decided to try his luck at fishing. He soon caught three big, beautiful fish.

Uncle Fox rushed home with his catch. "Aunt Fox, come and see what luck I've had today!" he called to his wife.

"Oh my! What huge fish!" cried Aunt Fox, licking her chops hungrily.

"You're right," said Uncle Fox. "You and I won't be able to eat all three of them. Why don't we invite Uncle Tiger to lunch? That would make him happy."

"Excellent, Uncle Fox," agreed Aunt Fox. "Go and invite Uncle Tiger. I'll fry the fish, and we'll have a wonderful meal!" Uncle Fox smiled and went off to find Uncle Tiger.

Aunt Fox put all three fish in a frying pan and placed them on the stove. The mouthwatering smell of fried fish floated through the house.

Aunt Fox's stomach began to grumble and growl. "I should try a piece of my fish," she thought to herself. "What if I didn't use enough salt? But I'll only eat a small piece. After all, it would be terrible if I ate up all my fish before Uncle Fox comes back."

Aunt Fox began nibbling at her fish. How tender and delicious it tasted! She forgot all about waiting for Uncle Fox and Uncle Tiger. In a few seconds, she had licked her plate clean.

"That was tasty!" Aunt Fox exclaimed. "Maybe I should try Uncle Fox's fish. He's very picky. If his fish isn't delightfully crispy and well-seasoned, I'm sure he'll be upset."

So Aunt Fox started nibbling at the second fish. First she ate the tail, then a fin, then the head. Before she knew it, Uncle Fox's fish was gone! "My goodness, I've eaten the whole thing!" Aunt Fox cried.

Now there was only one fish left. "Oh, well," murmured Aunt Fox. "The damage is done. I might as well eat the last one too."

And Aunt Fox gobbled up the third fish.

At last Uncle Fox arrived with Uncle Tiger. "Have you fried the fish?" Uncle Fox asked his wife.

"Of course I have!" she told him. "I put them by the fire so they wouldn't get cold."

"Well, serve them right away. We're starving. Right, Uncle Tiger?"

"Yes, Uncle Fox," agreed Uncle Tiger. "The fish smell so wonderful I can hardly wait to eat."

"Please sit here, Uncle Tiger," said Aunt Fox. "I will set the table."

"Thank you, Aunt Fox," said Uncle Tiger as he sat down.

Before Uncle Fox could sit down, Aunt Fox called him aside. "The fish were old and tough," she whispered. "They will be hard to cut. Go out to the patio and sharpen the knives."

Uncle Fox hurried outside. Soon Aunt Fox and Uncle Tiger could hear the harsh sound of Uncle Fox scraping knives against a stone.

Aunt Fox rushed over to Uncle Tiger. "Do you hear that?" she cried. "That's my husband, sharpening a knife. He's gone crazy! He told me he wants to eat your ears, Uncle Tiger! That's why he invited you for lunch. Run — before he comes back inside!"

Terrified, Uncle Tiger raced out of the house. Just then, Aunt Fox shouted, "Uncle Fox! Uncle Fox! Come quickly! Uncle Tiger has stolen all our fish!"

Uncle Fox dashed after Uncle Tiger. "Uncle Tiger, Uncle Tiger, please come back!" he begged. "Let me have at least one of them!"

Uncle Tiger, who thought Uncle Fox was begging for his ears, fled in fear. Faster and faster he ran. And he didn't stop until he reached his home, safe and sound.

Creating

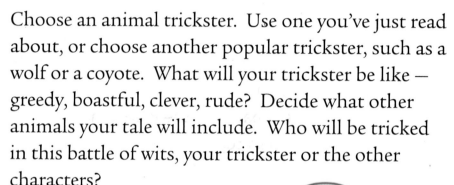

Write Your Own Trickster Tale

Choose an animal trickster. Use one you've just read about, or choose another popular trickster, such as a wolf or a coyote. What will your trickster be like — greedy, boastful, clever, rude? Decide what other animals your tale will include. Who will be tricked in this battle of wits, your trickster or the other characters?

Tips

- Use a story map to organize the elements of your tale.
- Introduce the characters, the setting, and the problem in a few sentences.
- Keep the events of the plot quick and simple.
- Write lots of lively dialogue.

Try These Trickster Treats

Brother Rabbit: A Cambodian Tale

by Minfong Ho and Saphan Ros (Lothrop)
A crocodile, two elephants, and a woman are no match for sneaky Brother Rabbit.

Borreguita and the Coyote: A Tale from Ayutla, Mexico

by Verna Aardema (Knopf)
A clever lamb uses her head, in more ways than one, to outsmart a foolish coyote.

The Flying Tortoise: An Igbo Tale

by Tololwa M. Mollel (Clarion)
A trip to Skyland lands Mbeku the greedy tortoise in a heap of trouble.

Zorro and Quwi: Tales of a Trickster Guinea Pig

by Rebecca Hickox (Bantam)
Quwi the guinea pig refuses to be a meal for a hungry fox.

Incredible STORIES

Read ... Think ... Dream

Ride me the waves
        of a story,
Settle me down
        by a brook,
Dream me a land
        only dreamed of,
Book me a voyage
        by book.

J. Patrick Lewis

Incredible STORIES

Contents

Reader's Library

- **Robocat**
- **The Dragon of Krakow**
- **My Green Thumb**
- **Luna**

Theme Paperbacks

Mouse Soup
written and illustrated by Arnold Lobel

Mufaro's Beautiful Daughters
written and illustrated by John Steptoe

Charlotte's Web
by E. B. White, pictures by Garth Williams

Book Links

If you like . . .

Dogzilla
by Dav Pilkey

Then try . . .

Kat Kong

by Dav Pilkey (Harcourt)
Dr. Vincent Varmint and Rosie Rodent capture the dreaded Kat Kong and bring him back to Mousopolis.

Over the Moon

by Rachel Vail (Orchard)
When acting in a play, a cow who is supposed to jump over the moon just can't seem to get it right.

If you like . . .

The Mysterious Giant of Barletta
by Tomie dePaola

Then try . . .

Dinosaur Bob and His Adventures with the Family Lazardo

by William Joyce (Harper)
The Lazardo family returns from Africa with a dinosaur who becomes a baseball hero.

Flat Stanley

by Jeff Brown (Harper)
A bulletin board falls on Stanley Lambchop, and suddenly he's only half-an-inch thick — or thin.

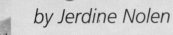

Dogzilla

MOVIE MONSTERS

Look out! Watching a huge **creature** destroy everything in its path can be **terrifying**, even if it's only make-believe. That's what makes movie monsters both **horrifying** and fun to watch.

A movie monster uses its **tremendous** strength and size to scare everyone. To defeat a monster, people must be smart and brave. They must do **heroic** things to save themselves, their town, and maybe even the world. They can do it, though. And it's all just good, scary fun.

A movie monster surprises these boys in 1954.

The story you are about to read is based on a famous movie monster named Godzilla. Godzilla is a colossal, 300-foot-tall, fire-breathing lizard.

It's Alive! GODZILLA KING OF THE MONSTERS! RAYMOND BURR

Godzilla first appeared in the movies in 1954. His monstrous size and loud roar still frighten people today.

Written and directed by
DAV PILKEY

The author calls this story "extremely goofy." Do you agree with him? **Evaluate** how well he uses the words and pictures to make you feel this way.

The stars of *Dogzilla* are the author's pets.
No harm came to any of the animals during the making of this book.

Starring

FLASH
as the Big Cheese

RABIES
*as Professor
Scarlett O'Hairy*

*Special
appearance by*
DWAYNE
as the Soldier Guy

LEIA
as the Monster

EG	THIS BOOK HAS BEEN RATED
	EXTREMELY GOOFY
	Some material may be too goofy for grown-ups.

It was summertime in the city of Mousopolis,

and mice from all corners of the community had come together
to compete in the First Annual Barbecue Cook-Off.

As the cook-off got under way, smoke from the
hot grills lifted the irresistible scent of barbecue sauce
over the roof-tops of the city.

A gentle wind carried the mouth-watering smell
into the distance, right over the top of an ancient crater.
Before long, a strange and mysterious sound was heard:
"Sniff . . . sniff. Sniff . . . sniff sniff sniff sniff . . ."

All at once, the volcano began to tremble.

And suddenly, up from the very depths of the earth
came the most terrifying creature ever known to mousekind:
the dreadful Dogzilla!

Immediately, soldiers were sent out to stop the mighty beast. The heroic troops were led by their brave commanding officer, the Big Cheese.

"All right, you old fleabag," squeaked the Big Cheese, "get those paws in the air — you're coming with us!"

Without warning, the monstrous mutt breathed her horrible breath onto the mice.

"Doggy breath!" screamed the soldiers. "Run for your lives!"

"Hey, come back here," shouted the Big Cheese to his troops. "What are you, men or mice?"

"We're MICE," they squeaked.

"Hmmmm," said the Big Cheese, "you're *right!* . . . Wait for me!"

The colossal canine followed the soldiers back to Mousopolis, licking up all of the food in her path.

Afterward, Dogzilla wandered through the city streets, doing those things that come naturally to dogs.

Dogzilla chased cars — right off the freeway!
Dogzilla chewed furniture — and the furniture store as well.
And Dogzilla dug up bones — at the Museum of Natural History.

Meanwhile, the Big Cheese had organized an emergency meeting with one of the city's greatest scientific minds, Professor Scarlett O'Hairy.

"Gentlemice," said Professor O'Hairy, "this monster comes from prehistoric times. It is perhaps millions of years old."

"Maybe we could teach it to do something positive for the community," suggested the Big Cheese.

"I'm afraid not," said Professor O'Hairy. "You simply *can't* teach an old dog new tricks!

"If we're going to defeat this dog, we've got to *think* like a dog! We've got to find something that *all* dogs are afraid of — something that will scare this beast away from Mousopolis FOREVER!"

"I've got an idea," squeaked the Big Cheese. . . .

Within minutes, the mice had assembled at the center of town.

"All right, Dogzilla," shouted the Big Cheese, "no more Mister Mice Guy — it's BATHTIME!"

Suddenly, a blast of warm, sudsy water hit Dogzilla with tremendous force.

The panicking pooch let out a burst of hot, fiery breath, and the chase was on!

The Big Cheese tried to catch up to the hot dog with all the relish he could muster.

Dogzilla hightailed it out of town, and back into the mouth of the ancient volcano.

"Well, I'll be dog-goned," squeaked the Big Cheese. "It worked!"

With the horrifying memory of the bubble bath etched in her mind forever, Dogzilla never again returned to Mousopolis.

Within a year, Mousopolis had rebuilt itself . . . just in time for the Second Annual Barbecue Cook-Off. The mice of Mousopolis fired up their grills, confident that they would never see or hear from Dogzilla again.

However, there was one thing they hadn't counted on . . .

Puppies!

Dav Pilkey has been playful all his life. When he was a baby, his parents would often hear him laughing in his sleep. When he got a little older and other kids were outside playing sports, Dav was inside drawing goofy pictures.

Today Pilkey spends his time making goofy books. One day while he was watching television, Leia, the dog, came charging into the room and knocked over a castle made out of blocks. "Leia looked like a silly monster who had just rampaged a city," Pilkey says. That smashing scene gave him the idea for *Dogzilla*.

Other books:
A Friend for Dragon, Dragon Gets By, Kat Kong

Internet

To find out more about Dav Pilkey, visit Education Place. **www.eduplace.com/kids**

Think About the Selection

1. How is Dogzilla like most real dogs? How is she not like a real dog?

2. How does thinking like a dog help the mice defeat Dogzilla?

3. What if bathtime hadn't scared Dogzilla away? What other plans could the Big Cheese have made to save Mousopolis?

4. What do you think will happen at the Second Annual Barbecue Cook-Off?

5. How would the story have been different if a colossal kitty had come out of the volcano instead of a dreadful dog?

6. **Connecting/Comparing** How does Dav Pilkey make this story so funny and incredible? Give examples from both the words and the pictures.

Persuading

Write a Movie Ad

Write an ad for a movie of *Dogzilla.* Draw an exciting scene from the story. Add the title and list the actors. Write sentences and quotations from people that will make others want to see the movie.

Tips

- Look at newspaper ads for ideas.
- Use colorful adjectives such as *greatest, silliest,* and *heroic.*

Figure Out the Sale Price

Look at the picture of Gonzales's Furniture store on page 275. Then look at the original prices of the furniture in the chart below. If the sale price of each piece of furniture were half of the original price, how much would each one cost?

Bonus Figure out the sale price of the items if they were one-third off.

Item	Original Price
sofa	$60
nightstand	$30
easy chair	$36
dresser	$48
mirror	$18
lamp	$24

Create Tongue Twisters

Find a phrase in the story in which each word has the same beginning sound. Use that phrase to write a whole sentence in which all the important words have that same beginning sound. Say your tongue twisters aloud as fast as possible.

Tips

- Before writing, make a list of words to choose from.
- Practice speaking slowly at first. Then speed up.

The dreadful Dogzilla did dozens of dirty deeds.

Internet

Post a Review

Paws up or paws down? Write a review of *Dogzilla* and post it on Education Place. **www.eduplace.com/kids**

Go with the Flow!

by Anne Prokos

Millions of years ago, volcanoes started out as holes or cracks in the Earth's crust. After thousands of eruptions, layers of lava hardened on top of one another. The layers turned into mountains.

Build your own volcano!

What You Need

- **Modeling clay**
- **Small empty can**
- **Piece of cardboard**
- **Baking soda**
- **Vinegar**
- **Teaspoon**
- **Glue**
- **Plastic houses from a board game**

1 Mold clay into a volcano shape. Leave an opening at the top for the empty can.

Here's what goes on beneath those mountains.

Rocks called strata melt below the Earth's crust. Gases and burned rock mix together to make hot magma.

Pressure causes magma to shoot out of volcanic craters or vents. When magma reaches the Earth's surface, it's called lava.

Gas and ashes from burned rock separate from the lava. The ashes form a cloud and fall toward the Earth.

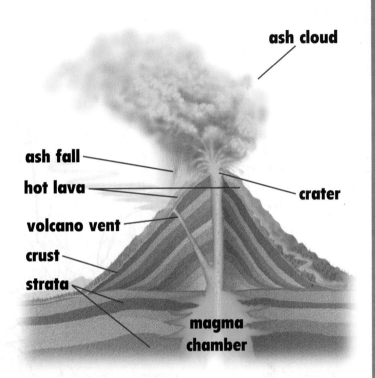

ash cloud

ash fall

hot lava

volcano vent

crust

strata

crater

magma chamber

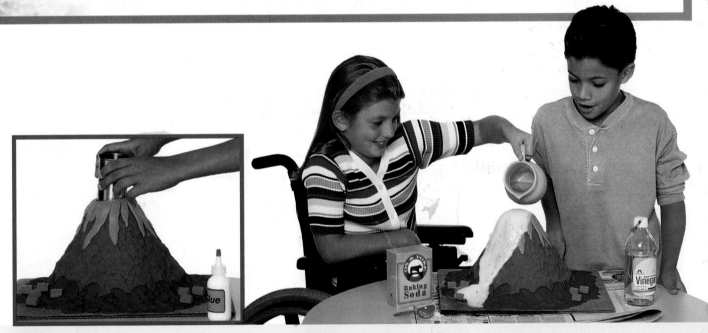

2 Insert the can into the "crater." Put your project on the cardboard and glue a few houses around your volcano.

3 Place one teaspoon of baking soda into the can. Add vinegar until it starts to foam. Watch where the "lava" flows.

A Story

A story tells about a true or fictional experience. It has a main character, and it has a beginning, a middle, and an end. Use this student's writing as a model when you write a story of your own.

Here I am with Pete.

Introducing the **characters** in a story usually takes place at the beginning.

A good description of the **setting** helps the reader to picture where the story takes place.

Pete, the Patriotic Pig

Pete was a patriotic pig. He said the Pledge of Allegiance every morning. He always dressed in red, white, and blue. His car was red, white, and blue too. Even his house was red, white, and blue.

Pete lived in Massachusetts. His job was to sing the National Anthem at the Boston Celtics basketball games. Everybody clapped and cheered after he sang. That made Pete feel really good.

One day Pete got bored with his job. He thought it would be fun to be an ice cream vendor instead.

So that day at the game he got the job to sell red, white, and blue ice cream. "Ice cream for sale! Ice cream for sale!" yelled Pete.

"My ice cream is melting!" screamed an angry fan.

"My ice cream is sour!" said another.

The job was not as much fun as Pete thought it would be. Nobody cheered for him or anything. Pete wanted his old job back.

The next day Pete got his old job back. He sang the National Anthem and everybody cheered. Pete was happy again.

A good **plot** makes the reader want to find out what will happen.

Using **dialogue** makes a story come alive.

A good **ending** wraps up the story.

Meet the Author

Eric D.
Grade: three
State: Massachusetts
Hobbies: soccer, reading
What he'd like to be when he grows up: a professional soccer player or a surgeon

A Mysterious STATUE

*A*bout 700 years ago, in 1309, a large **statue** of a young man washed up in the quiet harbor town of Barletta, Italy. No one knew where the statue had come from, but that didn't matter to the people of Barletta. They came to love the statue anyway.

Even today, the statue is **mysterious**. It stands on a **pedestal** in Barletta's town **square** and is almost eighteen feet tall. The statue looks strong and brave as it watches over the townspeople. The townspeople often tell stories about their beloved **giant**. One of their favorites is the story you are about to read.

This is the town of Barletta, Italy.

The mysterious giant watches over the town of Barletta from its pedestal in the square.

Standing next to the giant makes a person look like a tiny **weakling**.

Tomie dePaola

When Tomie dePaola was a boy, his Italian grandmother and Irish grandfather would tell him lots of old stories. As he listened, he began to dream of being an author. Today, in addition to writing his own stories, dePaola likes to retell old ones in his own words.

The Mysterious Giant of Barletta is one of those retellings. It is an Italian folktale. DePaola has retold Irish and Native American legends as well. Millions of children and adults enjoy the more than two hundred books he has illustrated and the nearly seventy he has written. To all his loyal fans, dePaola says "grazie — thank you."

OTHER BOOKS

Tony's Bread   Strega Nona

26 Fairmount Avenue   Days of the Blackbird

Jamie O'Rourke and the Big Potato

Internet

Visit Education Place and find out more about Tomie dePaola.
www.eduplace.com/kids

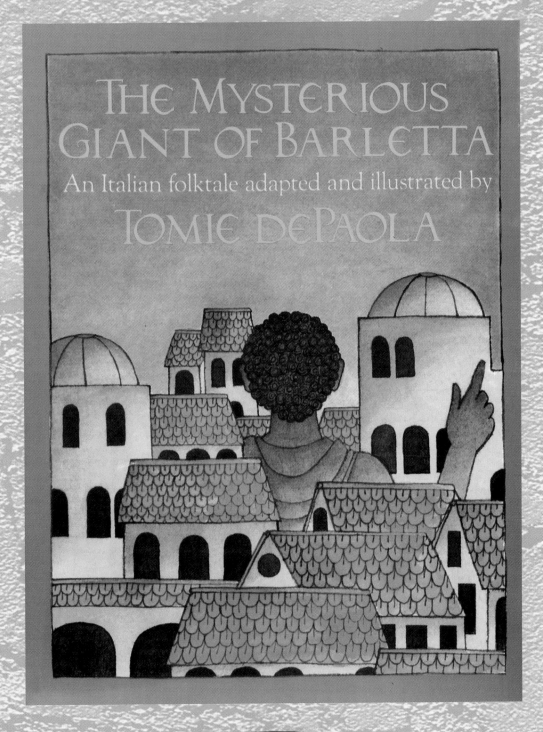

THE MYSTERIOUS GIANT OF BARLETTA

An Italian folktale adapted and illustrated by

TOMIE dePAOLA

As you read about Barletta and the giant, think of **questions** about the town, its people, and the strange events that happen there.

In the town of Barletta, in front of the Church of San Sepolcro, stood a huge statue. No one knew where it had come from or when. The Mysterious Giant — for that is what the people called the statue — had always been there as long as anyone could remember.

Even Zia Concetta [kahn-CHEHT-ta]. Zia Concetta was the oldest one in all of Barletta. She lived right across the square from the giant statue. "Every day, every night, for my whole lifetime, I've looked out the window and there he is," she would say.

Good weather and bad, the Mysterious Giant stood there. The people of Barletta loved having the statue in their town.

In the early morning, right before the sun came up, the sisters from the convent and other townspeople came to the church for Holy Mass. They always greeted the giant with a nod or a smile.

The people on the way to market always hailed the giant and asked that he give them good luck to sell all their goods or to get a good bargain.

All day long the children played around his legs, and the doves flew around his head. The young boys would sit on his big feet and tell jokes.

A little later the older boys would sit on the giant's feet to watch the older girls walk by. And at night, lovers would steal kisses in the giant's shadow.

Then the streets would be empty. Doves would settle on the giant's head and shoulders and arms and coo themselves to sleep, and Zia Concetta would open her window and call, *"Buona notte, Colosso — good night, Big One."*

This was the time the giant loved best. All was calm, all was still. *Ah, what a peaceful life,* the Mysterious Giant thought.

But one day this peaceful life was over. Word had reached the town that an army of a thousand men was destroying all the towns and cities along the lower Adriatic coast. And this army was heading straight for Barletta.

The townspeople ran through the streets in panic. No one in Barletta was ready for an army coming to destroy them. They had no generals, no captains. Why, they didn't even have any soldiers!

Shouts and screams echoed off the buildings. The night was lit by torches. All the peace and quiet was gone. No doves came to settle on the Mysterious Giant's shoulders, and Zia Concetta didn't call *"Buona notte"* from her window. The Mysterious Giant didn't like this at all.

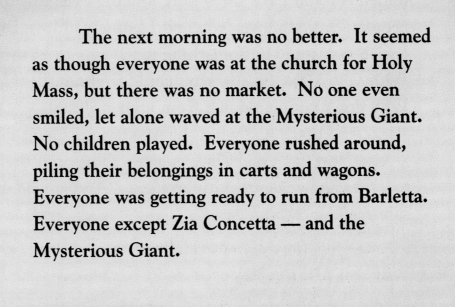

The next morning was no better. It seemed as though everyone was at the church for Holy Mass, but there was no market. No one even smiled, let alone waved at the Mysterious Giant. No children played. Everyone rushed around, piling their belongings in carts and wagons. Everyone was getting ready to run from Barletta. Everyone except Zia Concetta — and the Mysterious Giant.

"*Colosso*," she said to the huge statue, "as long as I can remember you have stood here looking over this town and its people. Barletta loves you and I know you love Barletta. I wish you could do something to save us from this army. With your size, I'm sure you could frighten them away. Why don't you hop down from your pedestal?"

And that's just what the Mysterious Giant did!

"Now . . ." said Zia Concetta. They put their heads together and came up with an idea. "And a good one, too," said Zia Concetta.

The Mysterious Giant climbed back and stood still. "People of Barletta," Zia Concetta called. "Come quickly! Great news . . . *un miracolo* — a miracle — our giant is going to save us. Come!"

The people of Barletta gathered around. "Friends," Zia Concetta said, "our giant will go to meet this army himself! All you have to do is three things. First, bring me the biggest onion you can find. Second, stay completely out of sight. Hide under the bed, hide in the closet, hide in the cellar, hide in the attic, but stay out of sight. And third — don't ask any questions! Have faith in our Mysterious Giant."

Someone quickly brought an onion. "Now, hide!" shouted Zia Concetta, and everyone scurried off.

"Well, *Colosso,*" said Zia Concetta as she sliced the onion in half, *"buona fortuna."* The Mysterious Giant took an onion half in each hand, once more stepped off the pedestal, and strode off to meet the army.

Three miles outside the city the Mysterious Giant sat down by the side of the road and held the onion pieces close to his eyes. Big tears began to run down his cheeks. The giant made loud sobbing noises.

What a sight the army saw as it came over the hill! "Halt," shouted the captain. The army halted. "What is that?" the captain whispered to one of his lieutenants.

"It looks like a giant boy — crying," answered the lieutenant.

"Well, we'll see about this," said the captain, marching off to where the Mysterious Giant sat.

"I am Captain Minckion," the captain declared. "We have come to destroy this town. Who are you, and what are you doing here crying? No tricks now — answer me!"

"Oh, sir," said the giant, sobbing, "I'm sitting out here, away from the town, because the other boys in school won't let me play with them. They say I'm too small. They pick on me all the time. They call me names, like *minuscolo* and *debole* — 'tiny' and 'weakling.' I'm always the last one chosen for games. Today they told me that if I tried to go to school they would beat me up. I hate being so small."

The giant sniffed loudly and blew the hats off the soldiers standing in front. The captain and the army stood dumbstruck. If this giant was a small boy that the others teased, then imagine what the rest of the people of this town were like.

"But someday, sir," the giant bellowed, "someday, I'll show them. I'm going to eat up all my pasta, and I'll grow big and strong, and then I'll be able to fight back."

The soldiers began to back away, trembling. The
lieutenants gathered around the captain, who had backed
away from the giant, too. There was only one thing to do.
Captain Minckion and his lieutenants drew their swords.
They held them in the air and shouted . . .

"About-face! Double time — march!" The army
turned and fairly ran in the opposite direction of Barletta.
The Mysterious Giant threw away the onion halves, dried
his tears, and went back to the Church of San Sepolcro.

"They're gone," shouted Zia Concetta to the townspeople, as the giant climbed back on his pedestal once more. "The army is gone. You can come out now. The town has been saved. Our giant did it!"

Che bella festa! What a celebration was held that night!

But when it was over and the moon was high in the sky, the Mysterious Giant looked out over the sleeping town. Doves cooed themselves to sleep on his head and his shoulders.

Everything was calm, everything was still. Zia Concetta opened her window.

"*Buona notte, Colosso,*" she called, "and *grazie.*"

Think About the Selection

1. When all the townspeople get ready to run from Barletta, why is Zia Concetta the only one who doesn't panic?

2. Why do you think the Mysterious Giant decides to help Zia Concetta and the town?

3. Why does Zia Concetta ask the townspeople to stay out of sight? What might have happened if they hadn't followed her orders?

4. Why is it better for the Giant to trick the soldiers rather than to fight them?

5. If the Mysterious Giant came to *your* town, what could he help the people do?

6. **Connecting/Comparing** Suppose the Big Cheese from Mousopolis were in charge of saving Barletta. What might his plan have been?

Expressing

Write a Postcard

If you were visiting Barletta, what would you write to a friend? On one side of an index card, write your friend's address and a short message. Compare Barletta with your hometown. On the other side of the card, draw a scene from Barletta.

Tips

- To get started, list places and people in Barletta.
- Include your friend's name, street address, city, state, and ZIP code.

310

Make a Map

How well do you know Barletta? Draw a map of the town. Put the town square at the center. Show all the important places you read about in the story. Label the places clearly. Don't forget the statue of the Giant!

Bonus **Make a mileage scale for your map.**

Make an Italian Phrase Book

Write all the Italian words and phrases from the story on separate pieces of paper. Then put them in alphabetical order. Write the English meaning on each page and draw a picture that shows the meaning. Bind the pages together. *Buon divertimento!* Have fun!

Internet

Complete a Web Word Scramble

How fast can you unscramble a word? Test your skills on words from *The Mysterious Giant of Barletta*. Visit Education Place today!

www.eduplace.com/kids

**Skill: How to
Read a Social
Studies Article**

Before you read . . .

❶ **Read** the title
and heading.

❷ **Look at** photos
and captions.

❸ **Predict** what
you will learn.

While you read . . .

❶ **Identify** the time
and place the
article tells
about.

❷ **Identify** the main
idea of each
paragraph.

❸ **Take notes**
to help you
remember
what you
read.

EYES

Where can you see ancient ruins, eat authentic spaghetti, and visit the Vatican, the world's smallest state, in one day? Head for Rome, Italy's capital. Grab your travel gear and *avanti* — "go."

Called the "Eternal City" because of its long history, Rome was founded, legend says, in 753 B.C. Later it was the seat of the Roman Empire. Today you'll find many remains of the past here. "There are lots of old monuments, statues, and museums," says Matteo Ferrucci, 13. "My favorite statue is one of the emperor Marcus Aurelius on his horse." Livia Bianchini, 13, favors monuments called obelisks. These tall stone pillars decorate many public spaces.

"There are so many different things to do in Rome that it's hard to get bored," says Francesco Pannarale, 12. "If you want to learn history, go to see the Colosseum and the Roman Forum. For a great view of the city, go to Zodiaco." That's a café on a hill in the northwest section of the city. "From Zodiaco you can see at least half of Rome," Francesco says. "There's also a *gelateria* [ice cream shop] there!"

on ROME

by M. Linda Lee

▲ **DWARFED** by a giant head and hand, Francesco examines part of a statue at the Conservators' Palace Museum in Rome, Italy, where he lives. "The pieces are huge," says Francesco. "I can imagine how the whole statue must have looked in ancient times."

JUST LION AROUND. Matteo Ferrucci, 13, hams it up with a water-spouting marble lion at the Piazza del Popolo. The piazza [pea-AHT-zah], or square, is one of the largest in the city.

What do Roman teens do for fun? "I often go to Luna Park with my friends or family," says Matteo. "Luna Park is an amusement park with lots of rides." Francesco, Livia, and Matteo all recommend the park at Villa Borghese [bohr-GAY-zay], a former 17th-century estate where you'll find museums, galleries, and a zoo. "There are great bike trails around the little lake," says Francesco. And you can go horseback riding.

No one can quite put a finger on what makes Rome so special. According to Matteo, who lived in New York City for several years, "Rome and New York both have interesting museums, but Rome has more history." Adds Francesco, "People come to Rome to see the old sights, but there are lots of modern things to see, too." Livia agrees. "Rome is *molto bella* [very beautiful]," she says. "It's the best city in the world!"

TWO TOSSES. At the Trevi Fountain, custom says to toss one coin over your shoulder into the water so you'll return to Rome. A second toss grants a wish.

▼ **TRUTH OR CONSEQUENCES.**
Bocca della Verità, the Mouth of Truth, puts Francesco to the test. An old legend says that the mouth will "bite" the hand of anyone who tells a lie.

Raising
Dragons

WRITTEN BY
Jerdine Nolen

ILLUSTRATED BY
Elise Primavera

Working
on the Farm

On a farm, there are many **chores** to do. Raising crops and taking care of all the animals is hard work. Before you read the story *Raising Dragons,* you might want to know what it's like to live on a real farm. Here are some things a good farmer does.

Farmers **plow** the soil with the help of tractors. This tractor is **hitched** to a special tool that breaks up the dirt.

316

This girl is feeding a calf. After she has **tended** this calf, she may have other animals to care for as well.

Seeds are **sown** over the ground. Once the seeds grow into plants, they must be tended until the crops are ready to pick.

After the crops are **harvested**, there is plenty of food to eat. That's just what you need when you've worked up a healthy **appetite** doing farm chores!

Meet the Author
JERDINE NOLEN

Where she grew up: Chicago, Illinois

Where she lives now: Ellicott City, Maryland

Where she gets her ideas for books: She says she gets them from her children, from her cats, and even while she's doing laundry.

Fun fact: Her book *Harvey Potter's Balloon Farm* was made into a TV movie.

Other books: *Harvey Potter's Balloon Farm, In My Momma's Kitchen, Irene's Wish*

Meet the Illustrator
ELISE PRIMAVERA

Where she grew up: Long Branch, New Jersey

Where she lives now: Monmouth Beach, New Jersey

First thing she learned to draw: A tree. Her brother taught her when she was six years old.

Where she gets her ideas for books: She says her best ideas come to her when she's in the shower.

Do you want to find out more about Jerdine Nolen and Elise Primavera? Try visiting Education Place.

www.eduplace.com/kids

318

Raising Dragons

WRITTEN BY
Jerdine Nolen

ILLUSTRATED BY
Elise Primavera

Use what you know about farms, animals, and make-believe to **predict** what might happen when a little girl tries to raise a dragon on her family's farm.

Pa didn't know a thing about raising dragons. He raised corn and peas and barley and wheat. He raised sheep and cows and pigs and chickens. He raised just about everything we needed for life on our farm, but he didn't know a thing about raising dragons.

Ma didn't know about dragons, either. She made a real nice home for us. But when it came to dragons, she didn't even know what they wanted for dessert!

Now me, I knew everything about dragons, and I knew they were real.

At first Pa thought the notion of dragons on a farm was just plain foolishness. "I'm not too particular about fanciful critters. And, I don't have any time for make-believe," he told me one day. So when Pa said he didn't want to talk anymore, I knew I'd better keep my opinions to myself. I did my chores with my thoughts in my head at one end of the barn while Pa worked at the other end with his thoughts.

I remember the day my life with dragons began. I was out for my Sunday-before-supper walk. Near Miller's cave I came across something that looked like a big rock. But it was too round and too smooth — not hard enough to be a rock.

Carefully I rolled it into the cave and went to fetch Pa.

"What do you think it is, Pa?"

"An egg. A big egg," was all he said. "Now you stay away from that thing, daughter. No telling what'll come out of it!" I couldn't tell if Pa was more scared than worried. "You just stay away, you hear me!" he said, pointing a finger.

I always minded my parents, never had a reason not to. And I tried to mind Pa now, but I could not stay away. Day after day I'd go to Miller's cave to wait and watch, and wonder: *What is coming out of that egg?*

One night I couldn't sleep. I got out of my bed and climbed out of my window onto the perch Pa had made for me in the oak tree.

But a loud noise broke the stillness of the night. *Crack!* It was louder than one hundred firecrackers on the Fourth of July. *CRACK!* I heard it again, this time louder than before. It was coming from Miller's cave. At the first hint of dawn, I headed toward that sound.

There in the corner of the cave, where I'd left it, was the egg. And pushing its way out, like I've seen so many baby chicks do, was a tiny dragon poking through that shell with its snout.

It was love at first sight.

"Hey there, li'l feller, welcome to the world," I sang, soft and low. As I stroked his nose, a sweet little purring whimper came from him. As I touched skin to scale, I knew I was his girl and he was my dragon. I named him Hank.

Hank was just a joy to have around. He was a fire-breathing dragon, and he made sure he kept his temper whenever I was near.

Pa wouldn't have seen the sense or the use of having a dragon around who ate you out of house and home. Thankfully, Hank preferred fish, frogs, eels, and insects to beef, lamb, chicken, and pork. And he *did* have a healthy appetite!

Ma never wanted to know about Hank. Whenever I wanted to talk about him, she'd cover her ears and sing. She said that having a dragon around had to be worse than having a field full of critters. But it wasn't.

Ma and Pa taught me about caring for living creatures from the day I was born. They taught me about raising lots of things, but they never imagined I would someday care for a critter most folks don't even believe existed. It did take a little time, but whether they liked it or not, Hank was part of our lives.

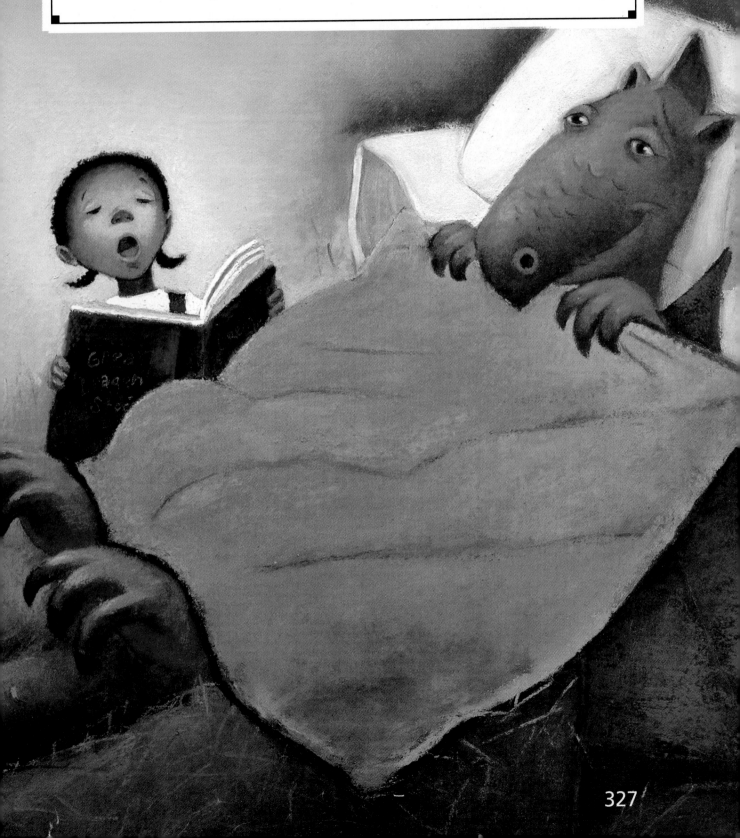

He was an awesome thing. Growing to be as big as the barn from tail to snout. Hank was very clumsy when his wings came in. But once he learned how to use them, we'd go flying, mostly at night.

Up until then I had been afraid of the dark. The shadows and muffled noises and the complete quiet stillness always seemed to be waiting and watching me. I had seen our farm from up in my tree perch. But Hank showed me my world from on high, the way a cloud or a bird or a star just might be seeing me. Up there I saw things for what they were. And it was just grand!

Pa was the first one to notice what he called a strangeness happening around our farm. One morning with Samson, our mule, hitched for work, Pa set out to plow the fields. But all the work had been done. The ground was turned over and seeds had been sown. Pa was plumb flabbergasted!

Hank and I tended the crops, too. We pulled weeds and kept varmints away. And Hank even got me to school before the first bell.

Even after all the good he'd done, Ma still didn't want any part of Hank. But when a hot spell hit, her tomatoes began to dry out. Hank hovered above them, fanning away the heat. He saved just about every last one of them. Ma didn't admit it, but she felt beholden to Hank. She began fixing fancy gourmet meals just for him — eel potpies, frog-leg pudding, and a fish-and-insect stew that Hank just loved.

Day by day Hank was getting bigger. Ma was uneasy about Hank's fire-breathing breath.

Pa paced with worry about all the corn Hank and I planted. There was corn growing *everywhere*. Ma cooked as much of it as she could, but there was too much. Just when it seemed like the corn would swallow up our farm, Hank grabbed Pa's shovel and dug a wide trench around the cornfield. Then he blew on it with his hot breath.

"What in tarnation?" Pa screamed. Ma ran out of the house carrying a bucket of water. But it was too late. The whole field was ablaze. We couldn't believe our ears — POP! POP!! Pop, Pop! POP! — or our eyes.

Hank was making popcorn. It took an entire week to salt and bag it. We sold it all — at a profit. It was the first dragon-popped popcorn anybody ever saw or tasted. Oh, it was *real* good, too.

When Ma harvested her tomatoes, Nancy Akins bought some. She claimed they had medicinal value. She said they cured her gout. Pretty soon folks wanted dragon-grown food like they wanted medicine. But there was nothing medicinal about it. It was just Hank.

The crowds and attention decided his fate. One evening Ma and I were sitting in front of our potbellied stove. She was shelling peas while I read *Murdoch's Adventure Atlas of the Known and Unknown World,* a book I'd gotten from the library that morning. In that instant I realized what I needed to do.

Come morning, Hank and I set out for the dragon-shaped landmass floating in the middle of the ocean.

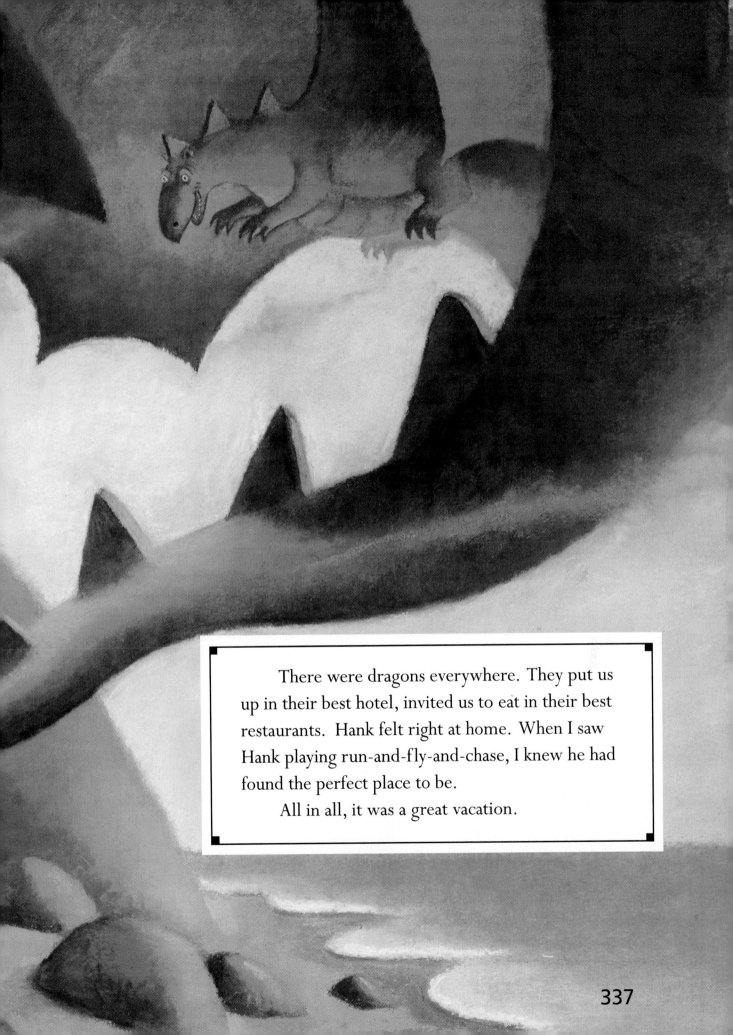

There were dragons everywhere. They put us up in their best hotel, invited us to eat in their best restaurants. Hank felt right at home. When I saw Hank playing run-and-fly-and-chase, I knew he had found the perfect place to be.

All in all, it was a great vacation.

338

But at the end, it got real hard: I had to say farewell to Hank. At least for now.

Normally I don't get mushy at departing, but when Hank turned to me and called me Cupcake, I *boohooed* a heap.

Just as I was about to board my plane, Hank stood there on the runway trying to hide a wheelbarrow behind his back. His toothy grin lit up that cloudy day. That wheelbarrow was full of . . .

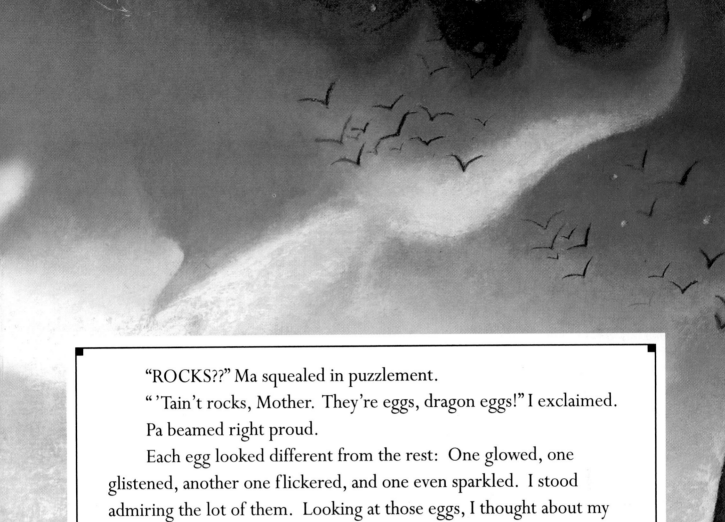

"ROCKS??" Ma squealed in puzzlement.

" 'Tain't rocks, Mother. They're eggs, dragon eggs!" I exclaimed.
Pa beamed right proud.

Each egg looked different from the rest: One glowed, one
glistened, another one flickered, and one even sparkled. I stood
admiring the lot of them. Looking at those eggs, I thought about my
Hank. For now, he was out there somewhere in the world. I knew I'd
see him again. Wondering *when* was the only thing fixed in my mind.

But in the meantime, I knew what I had to do. The same way
Pa knew that farming was in his blood, I knew that raising dragons
was in mine.

There are some things you just know.

THINK ABOUT THE SELECTION

1. Describe the little girl's personality. What is she like? Give examples from the story to support your answer.

2. Why does Hank have to leave the farm? How do you think he felt about leaving?

3. If the little girl had never found the egg in Miller's Cave, how would life on the farm have been different?

4. What do you think will happen when the little girl tries to raise a group of dragons instead of just one?

5. What kind of person does someone have to be to take good care of an animal? Give examples from the story.

6. **Connecting/Comparing** Hank was very helpful on the farm. What might have happened if Hank were more like Dogzilla?

WRITE A SEQUEL

A sequel to a story tells what happens after that first story ends. What might happen if the little girl went back to Dragon Island? What would she say to the dragons? Write a sequel using your ideas.

Tips

- Before writing, draw a picture of your ideas.
- Use quotation marks at the beginning and end of a person's exact words.

Science

MAKE A LIFE CYCLE CHART

Create a chart that shows the stages of Hank's life cycle. Begin with the egg that the little girl found. Draw pictures of the other stages in Hank's life.

Listening and Speaking

ROLE-PLAY A NEWS REPORT

In a small group, role-play a television reporter's news report from the farm. Decide who will be the reporter, the little girl, her parents, and Hank. Present the live interviews to the rest of the class.

Tips

- Watch a news report on TV for ideas.

- Prepare questions before doing the interviews.

TAKE AN ONLINE POLL

Have you ever raised a pet? What unusual pets do you or your friends have? Who is your favorite character in *Raising Dragons*? Take an Education Place online poll. **www.eduplace.com/kids**

Skill: How to Read a Science Article

Before you read . . .

1. **Read** the title, headings, and captions.

2. **Look at** the photos.

3. **Predict** what you will learn.

While you read . . .

1. **Identify** the main idea of each paragraph.

2. **Identify** special science words and facts.

3. **Take notes** to help you remember what you read.

Real-Life DRAGONS

by Robert Gray

▲ **FOREST DRAGON**

You can see why this little lizard got the name "dragon." It has more spikes than most make-believe dragons! It lives in the rainforests of Australia.

Usually when forest dragons stay still, they're hard to see. Their green scales help to hide them in the leaves.

But when a forest dragon wants to scare an enemy, it stretches out the yellow skin under its chin. Then it fights with its teeth and claws.

KOMODO DRAGON

The world's biggest lizards are also called dragons. No wonder — they can grow to be ten feet (three meters) long. And a Komodo almost looks as if it's breathing fire! As it walks along, its long forked tongue flicks in and out of its red mouth.

Komodos live on six tiny islands in Indonesia, a country north of Australia. Adult Komodos eat almost any small animal they can find, including smaller Komodo dragons.

And they're big enough to kill deer and water buffaloes, but they can't outrun them. Instead, they lie next to the animals' trails and strike out quickly to grab their prey.

If an animal gets away after being bitten, no problem. It will probably die in a day or two. That's because germs in the Komodo's saliva can cause a deadly infection. After the animal dies, it starts to smell rotten. And before long, a Komodo will follow the odor and find a delicious dead dinner.

With their spikes and scales and fierce looks, these real-life dragons are just

AMAZING!

A lizard in the air? How rare! These dragons from India and Southeast Asia can't really fly. But they can glide from tree to tree to chase insects or escape from enemies.

Their "wings" are made of skin stretched over their ribs. To glide, they spread their ribs out and jump off a branch. The stretched-out skin acts like a parachute as they float down to a lower branch. When a flying dragon lands, it tucks its ribs against its body, as if it were closing a paper fan.

Both the green basilisk and the common basilisk have crests. That's why these dragon lizards were named after the rooster-like basilisks of long ago.

Make-believe basilisks were supposed to be able to kill people by looking at them. But these dragon lizards from Central America can do something amazing too. By running super-fast on their hind legs, they can zip across the top of the water for a short distance. What a great getaway!

Real or Make-Believe?

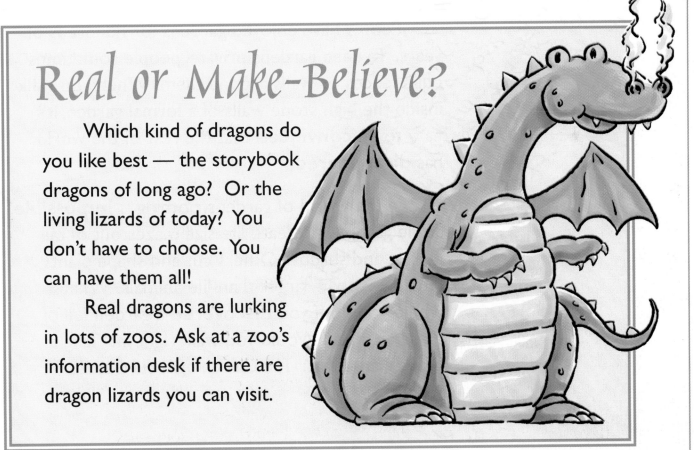

Which kind of dragons do you like best — the storybook dragons of long ago? Or the living lizards of today? You don't have to choose. You can have them all!

Real dragons are lurking in lots of zoos. Ask at a zoo's information desk if there are dragon lizards you can visit.

Unusual Gardens

People have enjoyed gardens for hundreds of years. To keep gardens private, people sometimes build fences or walls around them. When you walk inside the high stone walls of a formal garden, it's easy to be **convinced** that the rest of the world has **disappeared**.

In the world of gardens, nothing is **impossible**. Some gardeners create life-size mazes out of tall bushes and shrubs. Others cut and shape plants into **awesome**, larger-than-life animals. What would you do if you **discovered** a garden full of these animals? Would you walk right in? Take a chance, and enter *The Garden of Abdul Gasazi*.

A gardener's careful planning and clipping can create strange paths (above) and **incredible** leafy animals (below).

Meet the
Author and Illustrator
Chris Van Allsburg

Birthday: June 18

Favorite book as a child: *Harold and the Purple Crayon* by Crockett Johnson

Favorite subject in school: He loved art. Once, when he was sick, he wanted to go to school anyway because it was an art day.

His readers: He gets hundreds of letters from students. Some want a picture of him. Others want to invite him to dinner. They even ask him if he likes spaghetti.

His love of reading: He reads every word on the cereal box at breakfast, sometimes more than once.

Fun fact: His book *Jumanji* was made into a movie.

Other books:
Just a Dream
The Polar Express
Two Bad Ants
The Wreck of the Zephyr

Internet

You can find out more about Chris Van Allsburg at Education Place. **www.eduplace.com/kids**

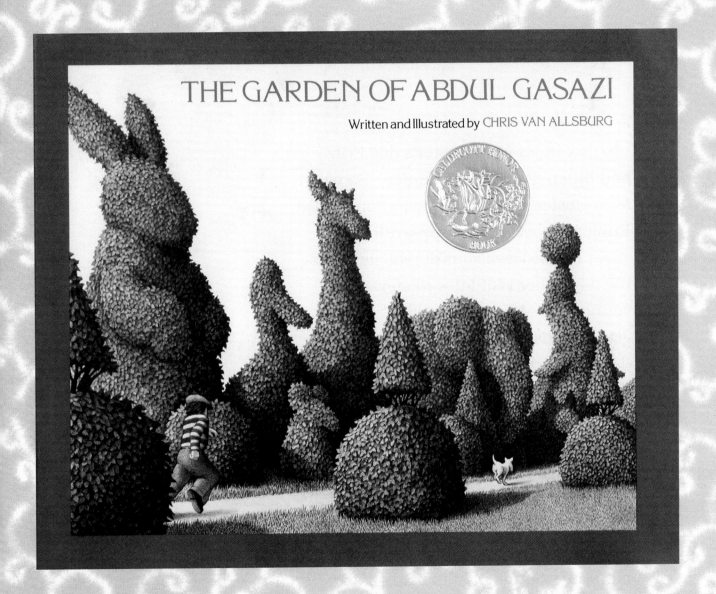

THE GARDEN OF ABDUL GASAZI

Written and Illustrated by CHRIS VAN ALLSBURG

Strategy Focus

As you follow the trail of incredible events in the story, pause to **monitor** your understanding. Reread or read ahead to **clarify** any clues along the way.

Six times Miss Hester's dog Fritz had bitten dear cousin Eunice. So when Miss Hester received an invitation to visit Eunice she was not surprised to read "P.S., Please leave your dog home." On the day of her visit Miss Hester asked young Alan Mitz to stay with Fritz and give him his afternoon walk.

As soon as Miss Hester left, Fritz ran into the parlor. He loved to chew on the chairs and shake the stuffing out of the pillows. But Alan was ready. All morning long he kept Fritz from sinking his sharp little teeth into the furniture. Finally the dog gave up and fell asleep, exhausted. Alan took a nap, too, but first he hid his hat under his shirt, hats being one of Fritz's favorite things to chew.

An hour later Alan quickly awoke when Fritz gave him a bite on the nose. The bad-mannered dog was ready for his afternoon walk. Alan fastened Fritz's leash and the dog dragged him out of the house. Walking along, they discovered a small white bridge at the side of the road. Alan decided to let Fritz lead the way across.

Some distance beyond the bridge Alan stopped to read a sign. It said: ABSOLUTELY, POSITIVELY NO DOGS ALLOWED IN THIS GARDEN. At the bottom it was signed: ABDUL GASAZI, RETIRED MAGICIAN. Behind the sign stood a vine-covered wall with an open doorway. Alan took the warning quite seriously. He turned to leave, but as he did, Fritz gave a tremendous tug and snapped right out of his collar. He bolted straight ahead through the open door, with Alan running right behind.

"Fritz, stop, you bad dog!" cried Alan, but the dog simply ignored him. Down shadowed paths and across sunlit lawns they raced, deeper and deeper into the garden. Finally, Alan drew close enough to grab hold of Fritz. But as he reached out he slipped and fell. Fritz barked with laughter as he galloped out of sight. Alan slowly picked himself up. He knew he had to find Fritz before Mr. Gasazi discovered him. Bruised and tired, he hurried off in the dog's direction.

After a long search Alan was ready to give up. He was afraid he might never find Fritz. But then he came upon fresh dog prints. Slowly he followed Fritz's tracks along a path that led into a forest. The dirt path ended and a brick walk began. There were no more tracks to follow, but Alan was certain that Fritz must be just ahead.

Alan started running. In front of him he could see a clearing in the forest. As he came dashing out of the woods he stopped as quickly as if he had run up against a wall. For there, in front of him, stood a truly awesome sight. It was the house of Gasazi. Alan nervously climbed the great stairs, convinced Fritz had come this way and been captured.

The boy's heart was pounding when he arrived at the huge
door. He took a deep breath and reached for the bell, but before
he touched it the door swung open. There, in the shadow of the
hallway, stood Gasazi the Great. "Greetings, do come in" was all
that he said.

Alan followed Gasazi into a large room. When the magician turned around Alan quickly apologized for letting Fritz into the garden. He politely asked that, if Mr. Gasazi had Fritz, would he please give him back? The magician listened carefully and then, smiling, said, "Certainly you may have your little Fritzie. Follow me." With those words he went to the door and led Alan back outside.

They were walking across the lawn when suddenly Gasazi stopped by a gathering of ducks. He began to speak in a voice that was more like a growl. "I detest dogs. They dig up my flowers, they chew on my trees. Do you know what I do to dogs I find in my garden?"

"What?" whispered Alan, almost afraid to hear the answer.

"I TURN THEM INTO DUCKS!" bellowed Gasazi.

In horror, Alan looked at the birds in front of him. When one duck came forward, Gasazi said, "There's your Fritz." Alan begged the magician to change Fritz back. "Impossible," he answered, "only time can do that. This spell may last years or perhaps just a day. Now take your dear bird and please don't come again."

When Alan took the bird in his arms it tried to give him a bite. "Good old boy," said Alan sadly as he patted the bird on the head. "You really haven't changed so much." With tears in his eyes he started for home. Behind him Alan could hear Gasazi laughing. As he approached the stairway, a gust of wind took Alan's hat sailing right off his head. Running along with one arm reaching for the hat, Alan lost his hold on Fritz. The duck flew out ahead and grabbed the hat in midair. But instead of landing he just kept on flying, higher and higher, until he disappeared in the afternoon clouds.

Alan just stood and stared at the empty sky. "Goodbye, old fellow," he called out sadly, sure that Fritz was gone forever. At least he had something to chew on. Slowly, one step after another, Alan found his way back to the garden gate and over the bridge. It was sunset by the time he reached Miss Hester's. Lights were on and he knew she must be home. With a heavy heart he approached the door, wondering how Miss Hester would take the news.

When Miss Hester came to the door Alan blurted out his incredible story. He could barely hold back the tears; then, racing out of the kitchen, dog food on his nose, came Fritz. Alan couldn't believe his eyes. "I'm afraid Mr. Gasazi played a trick on you," said Miss Hester, trying to hide a smile. "Fritz was in the front yard when I returned. He must have found his own way home while you were with Mr. Gasazi. You see, Alan, no one can really turn dogs into ducks; that old magician just made you think that duck was Fritz."

Alan felt very silly. He promised himself he'd never be fooled like that again. He was too old to believe in magic. Miss Hester watched from the porch as Alan waved goodbye and hurried down the road to go home. Then she called out to Fritz, who was playfully running around the front yard. He came trotting up the front steps with something in his mouth and dropped it at Miss Hester's feet. "Why you bad dog," she said. "What are you doing with Alan's hat?"

367

Think About the Selection

1. How would you describe Abdul Gasazi's personality? Use details from the story to make your point.

2. How do you think Fritz the dog ended up with Alan's hat?

3. Why does Miss Hester believe that Abdul Gasazi has played a trick on Alan? Do you agree with her?

4. How does Chris Van Allsburg make this story seem so mysterious? Give examples from the story.

5. Do you think Alan will ever go back into Abdul Gasazi's garden? Would *you* go into the garden if given the chance? Explain your answers.

6. **Connecting/Comparing** Compare Dragon Island in *Raising Dragons* to Abdul Gasazi's garden.

Reflecting

Write a Journal Entry

What a day Alan had! Write Alan's journal entry about his day with Fritz. Be sure to tell how he feels about Fritz, Abdul Gasazi, and all the day's strange events. Use exciting and mysterious details from the story.

Tips

- Before writing, make a list of the main events.
- Start the entry with a day and a date.

Role-Play a Dialogue

What if a dog you were taking care of ran into Abdul Gasazi's garden? With a partner, role-play a dialogue between yourself and Abdul Gasazi. What reasons could you give for getting the dog back? What would Abdul Gasazi say? Will you get back a dog or something else? You decide!

BUT THIS IS NOT MY DOG!

Tips

- **Write out your dialogue first.**
- **Practice with your partner.**

Compare Van Allsburg's Art

Choose a picture from *The Garden of Abdul Gasazi* and a picture from another book by Chris Van Allsburg. Compare the pictures. How are they alike? What can you tell about Van Allsburg's style from these pictures? Write your ideas and share them with the class.

from *The Stranger* by Chris Van Allsburg

Internet

Complete a Web Maze

Can you find your way out of Abdul Gasazi's garden? Print a maze from Education Place and try your luck. **www.eduplace.com/kids**

Skill: How to Read an Interview

① **Read** the title and the introduction.

② **Identify** who is being interviewed and who is asking the questions.

③ **Ask** yourself what you know about the person being interviewed.

④ As you read, **pause** to make sure you understand each question and answer.

Enter the World of CHRIS VAN ALLSBURG

by Stephanie Loer

The questions for this interview with Chris Van Allsburg came from students, teachers, and fans of his books.

Where do you get the ideas for your pictures and stories?

At first, I see pictures of a story in my mind. Then creating the story comes from asking questions of myself. I guess you might call it the "what if — and what then" approach to writing and illustration.

Polar Express started with the idea of a train standing alone in the woods. Then I began asking questions: What if a boy gets on the train? What does he do? Where does he go? After the boy got on, I tried different destinations out in my mind. What about north? Who lives in the north? Then ideas of Christmas, Santa Claus, and faith began to take shape.

Van Allsburg's ideas come to life in his sketches.

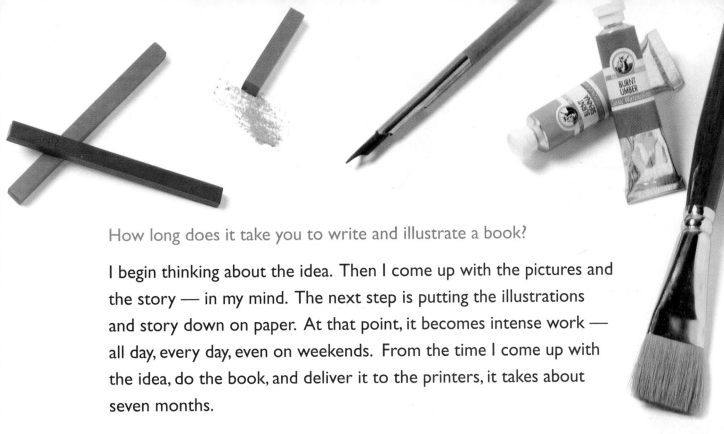

How long does it take you to write and illustrate a book?

I begin thinking about the idea. Then I come up with the pictures and the story — in my mind. The next step is putting the illustrations and story down on paper. At that point, it becomes intense work — all day, every day, even on weekends. From the time I come up with the idea, do the book, and deliver it to the printers, it takes about seven months.

Van Allsburg created sketches for his book *Jumanji*. Then he drew a complete outline (above) of each sketch and turned it into a finished illustration (right).

An ordinary train looks mysterious in this illustration from Van Allsburg's book _The Polar Express_.

How would you describe the artistic style in your books?

Think of it this way: Although the pictures look quite representational — like everyday, ordinary things — underlying this orderly look of the drawings there is a somewhat mysterious or puzzling quality.

In other words, the style I use allows me to make a drawing that has a little mystery to it, even if the actual things I am drawing are not strange or mysterious.

If you were to do a sequel, what books would you select?

My own interests might draw me to _The Widow's Broom,_ because the widow and the broom could have some more adventures. Also, _Two Bad Ants_ might get in trouble again in a different room. Or Alan could go back to Gasazi and get into more trouble with the magician.

So, I guess if I ever do run out of ideas — there's lots of material to fall back on. But I doubt if that will ever happen.

Van Allsburg started collecting plastic animals when he needed good models for _Jumanji_.

Focus on Fritz

No talk with Chris Van Allsburg would be complete without Fritz. While Chris does not own a dog, his brother-in-law once owned an English bull terrier very similar to Fritz. That dog (see below) served as an inspiration for *The Garden of Abdul Gasazi*. Since then, Fritz has appeared in almost all of Chris Van Allsburg's books, though sometimes he is hiding.

Can you find Fritz in every book? We don't want to give away all of Fritz's hiding places, but we will get you started. In *The Polar Express*, he is the puppet on the bedknob on the first page. Sorry, no more hints, but if you look close enough, you'll eventually find Fritz.

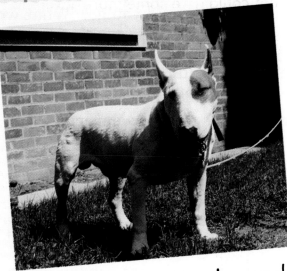

Enjoying the Backyard

✔ Writing a Personal Response

Some tests ask you to give a personal response to a topic. Often you have a choice of several topics. Here is a sample.

1. Write one or two paragraphs about one of the topics below.

a. Alan has an incredible adventure in the story *The Garden of Abdul Gasazi*. Think about an incredible adventure that you would like to have. Where would you go? What would you do? Why would this adventure be incredible?

b. You've just read the theme *Incredible Stories*. Do you like to read incredible fantasy stories? Give reasons for your answer.

_____

_____

_____

_____

Now look at a good response to the first topic that one student wrote.

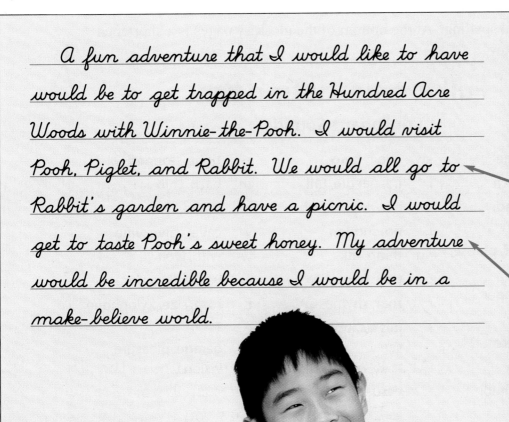

A fun adventure that I would like to have would be to get trapped in the Hundred Acre Woods with Winnie-the-Pooh. I would visit Pooh, Piglet, and Rabbit. We would all go to Rabbit's garden and have a picnic. I would get to taste Pooh's sweet honey. My adventure would be incredible because I would be in a make-believe world.

The response focuses on the topic throughout.

The response is well organized.

Many details support the response.

The response includes vivid and exact words.

There are almost no mistakes in capitalization, punctuation, grammar, or spelling.

Glossary

This glossary contains meanings and pronunciations for some of the words in this book. The Full Pronunciation Key shows how to pronounce each consonant and vowel in a special spelling. At the bottom of the glossary pages is a shortened form of the full key.

Full Pronunciation Key

Consonant Sounds

b	**bib**, ca**bb**age	kw	**ch**oir, **qu**ick	t	**t**igh**t**, stopp**ed**
ch	**ch**ur**ch**, sti**tch**	l	**l**id, need**l**e, ta**ll**	th	ba**th**, **th**in
d	**d**ee**d**, mail**ed**, pu**dd**le	m	a**m**, **m**an, du**mb**	*th*	ba**th**e, **th**is
f	**f**ast, **f**i**f**e, o**ff**, **ph**rase, rou**gh**	n	**n**o, sudd**en**	v	ca**v**e, val**v**e, **v**ine
		ng	thi**ng**, i**nk**	w	**w**ith, **w**olf
g	**g**a**g**, **g**et, fin**g**er	p	**p**o**p**, ha**pp**y	y	**y**es, **y**olk, on**i**on
h	**h**at, **wh**o	r	**r**oar, **rh**yme	z	ro**s**e, si**z**e, **x**ylophone, **z**ebra
hw	**wh**ich, **wh**ere	s	mi**ss**, **s**auce, **sc**ene, **s**ee		
j	**j**u**dg**e, **g**em	sh	di**sh**, **sh**ip, **s**ugar, ti**ss**ue	zh	gara**g**e, plea**s**ure, vi**s**ion
k	**c**at, **k**i**ck**, s**ch**ool				

Vowel Sounds

ă	p**a**t, l**au**gh	ŏ	h**o**rrible, p**o**t	ŭ	c**u**t, fl**oo**d, r**ou**gh, s**o**me
ā	**a**pe, **ai**d, p**ay**	ō	g**o**, r**ow**, t**oe**, th**ough**	û	c**ir**cle, f**ur**, h**ear**d, t**er**m, t**ur**n, **ur**ge, w**or**d
â	**ai**r, c**a**re, w**ear**	ô	**a**ll, c**au**ght, f**or**, p**aw**		
ä	f**a**ther, k**o**ala, y**a**rd	oi	b**oy**, n**oi**se, **oi**l		
ĕ	p**e**t, pl**ea**sure, **a**ny	ou	c**ow**, **ou**t	yŏŏ	c**u**re
ē	b**e**, b**ee**, **ea**sy, pian**o**	ŏŏ	f**u**ll, b**oo**k, w**o**lf	yōō	ab**u**se, **u**se
ĭ	**i**f, p**i**t, b**u**sy	ōō	b**oo**t, r**u**de, fr**ui**t, fl**ew**	ə	**a**go, sil**e**nt, penc**i**l, lem**o**n, circ**u**s
ī	r**i**de, b**y**, p**ie**, h**igh**				
î	d**ear**, d**eer**, f**ier**ce, m**ere**				

Stress Marks

Primary Stress ´: bi·ol·o·gy [bī **ŏl**´ ə jē]
Secondary Stress ´: bi·o·log·i·cal [bī´ ə **lŏj**´ ĭ kəl]

Pronunciation key and definitions © 1998 by Houghton Mifflin Company. Adapted and reprinted by permission from *The American Heritage Children's Dictionary*.

376

A

an·ces·tor (ăn´ sĕs´ tər) *noun*
A person one's family comes from: *Helen and her parents were born in the United States, but their **ancestors** were born in China.*

ap·pe·tite (ăp´ ĭ tīt´) *noun*
The desire for food: *The larger the puppy grew, the bigger its **appetite** became.*

ar·mor (är´ mər) *noun* A heavy covering, often of metal, worn to protect the body in battle: *The soldier put on **armor** before the battle began.*

awe·some (ô´ səm) *adjective*
Causing a feeling of wonder, fear, and respect: *John was amazed by the **awesome** sight of the old castle.*

B

bor·der (bôr´ dər) *noun*
A part that forms the outside edge of something: *There was a lace **border** around the edge of the tablecloth.*

boul·der (bōl´ dər) *noun*
A large rounded rock: *We crossed the stream by stepping on the **boulders** sticking out of the water.*

C

can·yon (kăn´ yən) *noun*
A deep valley with steep walls on both sides that was formed by running water: *The Grand **Canyon** was formed by the Colorado River millions of years ago.*

caul·dron also **cal·dron** (kôl´ drən) *noun* A large pot or kettle used for boiling: *The camp cook served hot soup from a steaming **cauldron**.*

ce·leb·ri·ty (sə lĕb´ rĭ tē) *noun*
A famous person: *Marta asked the **celebrity** for her autograph.*

chore (chôr) *noun* A small job, usually done on a regular schedule: *Rachel's daily **chores** include washing the dishes and walking the dog.*

col·lec·tion (kə lĕk´ shən) *noun* A group of objects gathered together and saved, sometimes for display or study: *Paul has a **collection** of coins from around the world.*

co·los·sal (kə lŏs´ əl) *adjective*
Very big; enormous: *An elephant is **colossal** compared to a mouse.*

com·rade (kŏm´ răd´) *noun*
A companion, especially one who shares one's activities: *Rosa's **comrades** on the swim team cheered when she won the race.*

armor

Canyon
Canyon comes from the Spanish word *cañón,* meaning "a large tube or funnel."

Comrade
Spanish soldiers used to live in rooms called *camaradas.* Soldiers who shared a room called each other *camaradas.* In time, this became the English word *comrade.*

ōō b**oo**t / ou **ou**t / ŭ c**u**t / û f**u**r / hw **wh**ich / th **th**in / *th* **th**is / zh vi**si**on / ə **a**go, sil**e**nt, penc**i**l, lem**o**n, circ**u**s

377

con·vince (kən **vĭns´**) *verb*
To cause to do or believe
something; to make feel
certain: *Because the door was
open, Sasha was convinced
that his little sister had been
in his room.*

crea·ture (**krē´** chər) *noun*
A living being, especially an
animal: *Ruth's pet dog is a
friendly creature.*

D

di·rec·tion (dĭ **rĕk´** shən)
noun The line or path along
which someone or something
goes, lies, or points: *The
road split in three different
directions.*

dis·ap·pear (dĭs ə **pîr´**) *verb*
To pass out of sight; vanish:
*The sky became dark when the
sun disappeared behind some
clouds.*

dis·cov·er (dĭ **skŭv´** ər)
verb To find or learn: *When
Eric moved the branch, he
discovered a nest of birds
in the tree.*

E

el·der (**ĕl´** dər) *noun*
A person who is older: *Seth's
grandmother and grandfather
are the elders in the family.*

em·broi·der (ĕm **broi´** dər)
verb To decorate by sewing
designs with a needle and
thread: *The red flowers were
embroidered on the cloth.*

en·dure (ĕn **door´**) *or* (ĕn
dyoor´) *verb* To put up with;
to bear: *Julia endured the rain
and cold during her camping
trip.*

ex·hi·bi·tion (ĕk sə **bĭsh´** ən)
noun A display for the public:
*Tanya practiced her kicks for
the karate exhibition.*

ex·pert (**ĕk´** spûrt´) *noun*
A person who has great
knowledge or skill in a
special area: *My basketball
coaches are experts at
shooting and passing
the ball.*

F

fare·well (fâr **wĕl´**) *noun*
Good wishes at parting: *Jared
said farewell to his neighbors
before he left for vacation.*

flour·ish (**flûr´** ĭsh) *noun* An
energetic or dramatic waving
motion: *Scott unrolled the new
flag with a flourish.*

Elder
Elder comes
from the same
Old English
word as *old*.

embroider

ă **rat** / ā **pay** / â **care** / ä **father** / ĕ **pet** / ē **be** / ĭ **pit** / ī **pie** / î **fierce** / ŏ **pot** /
ō **go** / ô **paw, for** / oi **oil** / oŏ **book**

gath·er·ing (**găth´** ər ĭng)
noun A coming together
of people: *The family
gathering included parents,
grandparents, and children.*

giant (jī´ ənt) *noun* A huge,
very strong, imaginary creature
that looks like a human being.
—*adjective* Extremely large;
huge: *The **giant** pizza was big
enough to feed twenty people.*

H

har·vest (**här´** vĭst) *verb* To
gather or pick: *We **harvested**
the ripe apples from our tree
and baked an apple pie.*

he·ro·ic (hĭ **rō´** ĭk) *adjective*
Very brave or daring: *The
firefighter was famous for
his **heroic** rescues.*

hitch (hĭch) *verb* To tie or
fasten: *We **hitched** our horse,
Fred, to the wagon so he could
pull it.*

hon·or (**ŏn´** ər) *noun* Special
respect for excellence. —*verb*
To show special respect for:
*We will **honor** our teacher by
giving her an award.*

hor·ri·fy·ing (**hôr´** ə fī´ ĭng)
adjective Causing much fear:
*I liked riding the roller coaster,
but Kevin thought it was
horrifying.*

im·i·tate (**ĭm´** ĭ tāt´) *verb* To
copy the actions, looks, or
sounds of: *Anna learned the
dance by **imitating** her sister.*

im·pos·si·ble (ĭm **pŏs´** ə bəl)
adjective Not able to happen
or exist: *It is **impossible** to
turn straw into gold.*

in·cred·i·ble (ĭn **krĕd´** ə bəl)
adjective **1.** Too unlikely to
be believed. **2.** Astonishing
or amazing: *No one would
believe Leah's **incredible** story
about a talking fish.*

L

ledge (lĕj) *noun* A flat space
like a shelf on the side of a
cliff or rock wall: *The rock
climber rested on a **ledge**
halfway up the cliff.*

M

mon·strous (**mŏn´** strəs)
adjective Extremely large;
enormous: *The rowboat
looked tiny next to the
monstrous ship.*

mys·te·ri·ous (mĭ **stîr´** ē əs)
adjective Very hard to explain
or understand: *No one could
explain the **mysterious** egg on
the teacher's desk.*

harvest

hitch

ōō b**oo**t / ou **ou**t / ŭ **cu**t / û f**u**r / hw **wh**ich / th **th**in / th **th**is / zh vi**si**on /
ə **a**go, sil**e**nt, penc**i**l, lem**o**n, circ**u**s

379

N

nee·dle (nēd´ l) *noun*
A small, thin tool for sewing.
It has a sharp point at one end
and a tiny hole called an eye
at the other end to put thread
through: *He used a **needle**
and thread to fix the hole in
his sock.*

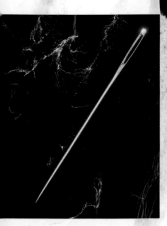

needle

plow

Rodeo
Rodeo comes
from the Spanish
word *rodear,*
meaning "to
surround."
A rodeo was
originally a
roundup of cattle
held once a year
on ranches. Over
time, it came to
mean a public
contest of cowboy
skills.

P

ped·es·tal (pĕd´ ĭ stəl) *noun*
A base or support, as for a
column or statue: *The Statue
of Liberty stands on top of a
pedestal.*

per·form·er (pər fôr´ mər)
noun A person who presents
a special talent or skill to an
audience: *We clapped for the
performers at the end of the
show.*

plow (plou) *verb* To break up
and turn over the soil with a
special tool: *The farmer had
to **plow** the fields before
planting seeds.*

R

rap·ids (răp´ ĭdz) *noun* A
group of small waterfalls in a
river where the water flows
very fast: *Our canoe trip was
peaceful until we reached the
rapids.*

re·spect (rĭ spĕkt´) *noun*
Admiration or consideration:
*Brian showed his **respect** for
nature by helping to clean up
the beach.* —*verb* To have or
show respect for.

ro·de·o (rō´ dē ō´) *or* (rō dā´ ō)
noun A public show of roping
and horseback riding skills:
*Everyone seemed to enjoy the
bronco riding at the **rodeo**.*

roy·al·ty (roi´ əl tē) *noun*
Members of a royal family,
such as kings, queens, princes,
or princesses: *The country's
royalty lived in the castle.*

rum·pled (rŭm´ pəld) *adjective*
Wrinkled: *Anita shook out her
rumpled coat after sitting on
it during the concert.*

S

scout (skout) *verb* To observe
or explore carefully to find
information: *Ada **scouted**
the trail to make sure it was
safe to hike.*

scraps (skrăps) *noun* Leftover
bits of cloth or other material:
*Manuel used **scraps** of colored
paper to create a picture.*

sew (sō) *verb* To make,
repair, or fasten something
with stitches, using a needle
and thread: *Suki's mother had
sewn Suki a bear costume for
the school play.*

ă rat / ā **p**ay / â **c**are / ä **f**ather / ĕ **p**et / ē **b**e / ĭ **p**it / ī **p**ie / î **f**ierce / ŏ **p**ot /
ō **g**o / ô **p**aw, for / oi **oil** / o͝o **b**ook

sheer (shîr) *adjective* Very steep: *The **sheer** rock wall rose straight up from the canyon floor.*

sit·u·a·tion (sĭch′ ōō ā′ shən) *noun* A set of conditions at a certain moment in time: *Freezing rain or thick fog can create dangerous **situations** for people who drive to work.*

sow (sō) *verb* To scatter seed over the ground for growing: *The seeds Amir had **sown** in the garden grew into pumpkins.*

square (skwâr) *noun* An open area in a city or town where two or more streets meet: *Jacob and Tony ate their lunch on a bench in the town **square**.*

stat·ue (stăch′ ōō) *noun* An image, often of a person or an animal, made out of something solid, such as stone or metal: *Gina saw a huge **statue** of Abraham Lincoln in Washington, D.C.*

sym·bol (sĭm′ bəl) *noun* Something that stands for or represents something else: *Each star on the United States flag is a **symbol** for one of the fifty states.*

T

tend (tĕnd) *verb* To look after; take care of: *Ben **tended** the garden by pulling weeds and watering the plants.*

ter·ri·fy·ing (tĕr′ ə fī′ ĭng) *adjective* Causing much fear: *The monster in the movie was a **terrifying** sight.*

thread (thrĕd) *verb* To pass thread through the eye of a needle or through the hooks and holes on a sewing machine: *Josh **threaded** a needle to sew the button back on his shirt.*

tre·men·dous (trĭ mĕn′ dəs) *adjective* Very great, large, or powerful: *Gloria swung the bat and hit the ball with **tremendous** force.*

tri·um·phant (trī ŭm′ fənt) *adjective* Successful: *The **triumphant** runner received a gold medal after the race.*

troop (trōōp) *noun* A group of soldiers: *The brave **troops** guarded the fort.*

U

un·u·su·al (ŭn yōō′ zhōō əl) *adjective* Not usual, common, or ordinary: *It is **unusual** for rain to fall in the desert.*

sow

statue

troop

ōō b**oo**t / ou **ou**t / ŭ c**u**t / û f**u**r / hw **wh**ich / th **th**in / *th* **th**is / zh vi**si**on / ə **a**go, sil**e**nt, penc**i**l, lem**o**n, circ**u**s

381

V

victorious

Weakling

Weakling contains the suffix *-ling,* which means "smaller or with less force." The suffix *-ling* also means "a person or animal that is young." Another word that contains *-ling* is *duckling.*

vic·to·ri·ous (vĭk tôr´ ē əs) *adjective* Having won by defeating another person or group: *The victorious soccer team celebrated after the game.*

vis·i·ble (vĭz´ ə bəl) *adjective* Able to be seen: *Beth's bright yellow jacket made her visible in the crowd.*

W

weak·ling (wēk´ lĭng) *noun* A person or animal without strength or power: *Compared to a lion, a house cat is a weakling.*

wealth (wĕlth) *noun* A great amount of money or valuable possessions: *The queen wore diamonds as a sign of her wealth.*

wor·ried (wûr´ ēd) *adjective* Feeling concerned or upset: *Tom was worried that the quarter would fall out of his pocket.*

ă rat / ā pay / â care / ä father / ĕ pet / ē be / ĭ pit / ī pie / î fierce / ŏ pot /
ō go / ô paw, for / oi oil / ŏŏ book

Acknowledgments

Main Literature Selections

Anthony Reynoso: Born to Rope, by Martha Cooper and Ginger Gordon. Text copyright © 1996 by Ginger Gordon. Photographs copyright © 1996 by Martha Cooper. Reprinted by permission of Houghton Mifflin Company. All rights reserved.

The Ballad of Mulan. This version of the traditional Chinese story of Mulan was written and illustrated by Song Nan Zhang, and published by Pan Asian Publications (USA) Inc., Union City, California. Copyright © 1998 by Song Nan Zhang. Reprinted by permission of the publisher.

Dancing Rainbows: A Pueblo Boy's Story, by Evelyn Clarke Mott. Copyright © 1996 by Evelyn Clarke Mott. Reprinted by permission of Dutton Children's Books, a division of Penguin Putnam Inc.

Dogzilla, by Dav Pilkey. Copyright © 1993 by Dav Pilkey. Reprinted by permission of Harcourt Inc.

The Garden of Abdul Gasazi, by Chris Van Allsburg. Copyright © 1979 by Chris Van Allsburg. Reprinted by permission of Houghton Mifflin Company. All rights reserved.

The Keeping Quilt, by Patricia Polacco. Copyright © 1998 by Patricia Polacco. Reprinted by permission of Simon & Schuster Books for Young Readers, an imprint of Simon & Schuster's Children's Publishing Division. All rights reserved.

The Lost and Found, by Mark Teague, published by Scholastic Press, a division of Scholastic Inc. Copyright © 1998 by Mark Teague. Reprinted by permission of Scholastic Inc.

The Mysterious Giant of Barletta, by Tomie dePaola. Copyright © 1984 by Tomie dePaola. Reprinted by permission of Harcourt Inc.

Raising Dragons, by Jerdine Nolen, illustrated by Elise Primavera. Text copyright © 1998 by Jerdine Nolen. Illustrations copyright © 1998 by Elise Primavera. Reprinted by permission of Harcourt Inc.

The Talking Cloth, by Rhonda Mitchell. Copyright © 1997 by Rhonda Mitchell. Reprinted by permission of Orchard Books, New York.

The Waterfall, by Jonathan London, illustrated by Jill Kastner. Text copyright © 1999 by Jonathan London. Illustrations copyright © 1999 by Jill Kastner. Reprinted by permission of Viking Children's Books, a division of Penguin Putnam Inc.

Focus on Trickster Tales Selections

"Aunt Fox and the Fried Fish," originally published as *"Tía Zorra y los peces"* in the anthology *El mundo de Tío Conejo* by Ediciones Ekaré, 1985. Text copyright © 1985 by Rafael Rivero Oramas. Reprinted by permission of the publisher.

"Hungry Spider," from *Thirty-Three Multicultural Tales to Tell*, by Pleasant L. DeSpain. Copyright © 1993 by Pleasant L. DeSpain. Reprinted by permission of August House Publishers, Inc.

"Rabbit Races with Turtle," from *How Rabbit Tricked Otter and Other Cherokee Trickster Stories*, by Gayle Ross. Copyright © 1994 by Gayle Ross. Reprinted by permission of *Parabola* magazine; www.parabola.org.

Links and Theme Openers

"Camping on the Wild Side," from the July 1997 issue of *Ranger Rick* magazine. Copyright © 1997 by the National Wildlife Federation. Reprinted by permission of the National Wildlife Federation.

"Chinese the Write Way," text by Susan Wills, illustrated by YongSheng Xuan, from the August 1996 issue of *Spider, the Magazine for Children*. Text copyright © by Susan Wills. Illustrations copyright © by YongSheng Xuan. Reprinted by permission of the author and illustrator.

"Eyes on Rome" from the July 1995 issue of *National Geographic World*. Copyright © 1995 by the National Geographic Society. Reprinted by permission of the publisher.

"Go with the Flow!" from the May 1997 issue of *3-2-1 Contact*. Copyright © 1997 by Children's Television Workshop. Reprinted by permission of the publisher.

"A Healthy Recipe from Ghana," originally published as *"Homemade Peanut Butter,"* from *The Kids' Multicultural Cookbook*, by Deanna F. Cook. Copyright © 1995 by Williamson Publishing. Reprinted by permission of the publisher.

"The House I Live In," words and music by Lewis Allen and Earl Robinson. Copyright © 1942 (Renewed) Chappell & Co., Inc. All rights reserved. Used by permission of Warner Bros. Publications, U.S. Inc., Miami, Florida.

"I Lost the Work I Found," from *The Goof Who Invented Homework and Other School Poems*, by Kalli Dakos, illustrated by Denise Brunkus. Text copyright © 1996 by Kalli Dakos. Reprinted by permission of Dial Books for Young Readers, a division of Penguin Putnam Inc.

"Lost," from *No More Homework! No More Tests! Kids' Favorite Funny School Poems*, edited by Bruce Lansky. Poem copyright © 1997 by Bruce Lansky. Reprinted by permission of Meadowbrook Press.

"Nesting Dolls," by Marie E. Kingdon, from *Hopscotch for Girls*, Vol. 10, No. 2, August/September 1998. Copyright © 1998 by Marie E. Kingdon. Reprinted by permission of the publisher.

"Rain and Rainbows," originally published as *"Rain of Color,"* from *The Science Book of Weather*, by Neil Ardley. Text copyright © 1992 by Neil Ardley. Copyright © 1992 by Dorling Kindersley Ltd., London. Reprinted by permission of Harcourt Inc.

"Read . . . Think . . . Dream," by J. Patrick Lewis. Copyright © 1992 by J. Patrick Lewis. Reprinted by permission of the author.

"Real-Life Dragons," originally published as *"Do You Believe in Dragons?"* by Robert Gray, from the October 1993 issue of *Ranger Rick* magazine. Copyright © 1993 by the National Wildlife Federation. Reprinted by permission of the publisher.

"September Yearning," from *Gingerbread Days*, by Joyce Carol Thomas. Copyright © 1995 by Joyce Carol Thomas. Illustrations copyright © 1995 by Floyd Cooper. Reprinted by permission of HarperCollins Publishers.

"Spotlight on Kids," originally published in *National Geographic World* magazine as the following: *"All That Jazz"* (March 1995 issue); *"Flamenco Fantástico"* (October 1996 issue); *"Musical Maestros . . . Relatively Speaking"* (May 1995 issue); and *"Talent with a Twist"* (June 1995 issue). Copyright © 1995, 1996 by the National Geographic Society. Reprinted by permission of the publisher.

Additional Acknowledgments

Special thanks to the following teachers whose students' compositions appear as Student Writing Models: Cindy Cheatwood, Florida; Diana Davis, North Carolina; Kathy Driscoll, Massachusetts; Linda Evers, Florida; Heidi Harrison, Michigan; Eileen Hoffman, Massachusetts; Bonnie Lewison, Florida; Kanetha McCord, Michigan.

Credits

Photography

3 (tr) image Copyright © 2000 PhotoDisc, Inc. **18** Michael Greenlar/Mercury Pictures. **54** (l) © Royal Ontario Museum/CORBIS. (br) © Seattle Art Museum/CORBIS. **55** (r)© Royal Ontario Museum/CORBIS. (b) © Keren Su/CORBIS. **56** Courtesy, Song Nan Zhang. **93** ©Graham French/Masterfile. **115** (t) Dennis Gray/Mercury Pictures. (b) Barry Korbman/Mercury Pictures. **119** © Roger Kaye. **120** (c) © Roger Kaye. **121** (tr) (l) © Roger Kaye. **124–5** "Statue of Liberty," 1986 © Milton Bond. **132** Lawrence Migdale. **156–7** Private Collection of Karen A. Fecko. **158** © Joseph Sohm; ChromoSohm Inc./CORBIS. **160** (c) Associated Press AP. **160–1** (b) © Panoramic Images. **161** (t) Associated Press AP. **162–78** © Martha Cooper. **179** (t) Courtesy, Ginger Gordon. (b) Courtesy, Martha Cooper. **182** © Caryn Levy. **183** Richard Nowitz/NGS Image Collection. **184** © Tamara Hoffer Photography. **185** Photograph by Gary Campbell ©. **186** © Lawrence Migdale/Mira. **187** (t) © Robert Frerck/Odyssey/Chicago. (b) © Margaret Courtney-Clark/CORBIS.

188 Kathie Lentz. **206** (banner) image Copyright © 2000 PhotoDisc, Inc. (l) © John Running. **207** (all) © Stephen Trimble. **208** Courtesy, Evelyn Clarke Mott. **209** (bkgd) image Copyright © 2000 PhotoDisc, Inc. **209–227** © Evelyn Clarke Mott. **230** image Copyright © 2000 PhotoDisc, Inc. **262** Corbis/Paul Kaye; Cordaiy Photo Library Ltd. **263** (t) Cinema Memories. (b) Movie Still Archives. **264–82** © Dav Pilkey. **283** Courtesy, Grolier Inc./Orchard Books. **286** (t) Corbis/Roger Ressmeyer. **290** (banner) image Copyright © 2000 PhotoDisc, Inc. (b) © F. Stella/Marka. **291** (t) © F. Stella/Marka. (b) © Giuliano Colliva/The Image Bank. **292** © Suki Coughlin. **313–15** (all) Richard Nowitz/NGS Image Collection. **316** (t) © Tony Stone Images/Curt Maas. (b) Larry Lefever/Grant Heilman Photography Inc. **317** (tl) (bl) Larry Lefever/Grant Heilman Photography Inc. **318** (t) Dennis Crews/Mercury Pictures. (b) Barry Korbman/Mercury Pictures. **344** © Hans & Judy Beste/Lochman Transparencies. **345** Masahiro Iijima/Nature Production. **346** (b) © Jean-Paul Ferrero/Auscape. **346–7** (t) Stephen Dalton/Animals Animals. **348** © Robin Shields/Mercury Pictures. **349** (t) Leo de Wys Inc./W. Hille. (b) © Robin Shields/Mercury Pictures. **350** Scott Goodwin Photography. **370–1** Scott Goodwin Photography. **371** (cl) sketch for *Jumanji* © Chris Van Allsburg. Courtesy of The Kerlan Collection, University of Minnesota. **373** Courtesy, Chris Van Allsburg. **377** ©Philadelphia Museum of Art/CORBIS. **378** © Morton Beebe, S.F./CORBIS. **379** (t) © Mark Gibson/CORBIS. (b) © Peter Turnley/CORBIS. **380** (t) © Randy Faris/CORBIS. (b) © Richard Hamilton Smith/CORBIS. **381** (t) © Lynda Richardson/CORBIS. (c) (b) © Kelly-Mooney Photography/CORBIS. **382** © TempSport/CORBIS.

Assignment Photography

372 (tl) Karen Ahola. **16–17, 46, 87** (r), **120** (bl), **130** (b), **131, 204, 231, 317** (r), **343** (r), **369** (l) Joel Benjamin. **286–7** (b) Kim Holcombe. **153** (ml, mr), **181** (ml), **203** (ml, mr), **229** (ml, mr) Jack Holtel. **123, 233, 375** Tony Scarpetta.

Illustration

48-49 Jean Hirashima. **51** Floyd Cooper. **89-90** Lily Toy Hong. **152** (bl) **228** (b) Mercedes McDonald. **230-231** Michael Sloan. **234** Mary Grandpré. **236-241, 254** (t) Daniel Moreton. **242-247, 254** (bl) copyright © 2001 by Murv Jacob. **248-253, 254** (br) Richard Bernal. **256-257** copyright © 2001 by Steve Johnson and Lou Fancher. **369, 371, 372** Chris Van Allsburg.